The Faber Book of Northern Folk-Tales

The Faber Book of
Northern Folk-Tales

EDITED BY
KEVIN CROSSLEY-HOLLAND

illustrated by Alan Howard

FABER AND FABER
London and Boston

First published in 1980
by Faber and Faber Limited
3 Queen Square, London WCIN 3AU
Printed and bound in Great Britain by
Fakenham Press Limited, Fakenham, Norfolk

British Library Cataloguing in Publication Data

The Faber book of Northern folktales.
1. Tales, European
2. Tales, Northern European
I. Crossley-Holland, Kevin
398.2'1'094   GR135

ISBN 0-571-11519-5

for
ELIZABETH POULTON

This evening I promise you a tale which will remind you of nothing and of everything.

—*Goethe*

Contents

Sources and Acknowledgements

"The Water-Sprite and the Bear" is taken from *German Hero-Sagas and Folk-Tales* by Barbara Leonie Picard, published by the Oxford University Press, London, 1958. "A Stork is not Always a Stork" and "True and Untrue" come from *Scandinavian Legends and Folk-Tales* retold by Gwyn Jones © Oxford University Press 1956, and are reprinted by permission of the publishers. "The Wizards of the Vestmanna Isles" and "The Dead Man's Nightcap" come from *Icelandic Folktales and Legends* by Jacqueline Simpson (B. T. Batsford, London, 1972) and "Eiríkur Rescues a Woman from the Otherworld" is reprinted from *Legends of Icelandic Magicians* edited and translated by Jacqueline Simpson (pp. 62–6), Cambridge, 1975, by permission of The Folklore Society and Boydell and Brewer Ltd.

"The Juniper Tree" is taken from *Animal Stories* by Walter de la Mare (Faber & Faber, London, 1939) and reprinted by permission of the Literary Trustees of Walter de la Mare and The Society of Authors as their representative. "The Bremen Town Musicians" comes from *About Wise Men and Simpletons—Tales from Grimm* translated by Elizabeth Shub and published by Hamish Hamilton Ltd, London, 1972.

"Annie Norn and the Fin Folk" comes from *The Hogboon of Hell and other Strange Orkney Tales* by W. Towrie and Nancy Cutt (André Deutsch Ltd., London, 1979) and "Johnnie in the Cradle", collected by Hamish Henderson, is reprinted from *A Dictionary of British Folk-Tales* edited by Katharine Briggs (Routledge & Kegan Paul, London, 1970–1). "The Woman of the Sea" comes from *The Princess Splendour and Other Stories* retold by Helen Waddell and edited by Eileen Colwell © Longman Young Books 1969, and is reprinted by permission of Penguin Books Ltd.

"The Rich Farmer and the Poor Farmer", "The Ghost and the Money Chest" and "Door Prayer at Evening" all come from *Ghosts, Witchcraft and the Other World* by Alan Boucher (Iceland Review Library, Reykjavik, 1977). "The Old Troll of Big Mountain" and "The Troll Ride" by Anne Wahlenberg are reprinted from *Great Swedish Fairy Tales* translated by Holger Lundbergh, English Translation © 1973 by Dell Publishing Co.,

Inc., by permission of Chatto & Windus Ltd. and Delacorte Press/Seymour Lawrence.

Acknowledgements are due and gladly given to the holders of copyrights listed above for their kind permission to include material in this anthology. All the other stories in this book are out of copyright; the authors and, where appropriate, the translators are credited at the end of each tale.

This volume is one of a "pair" with *The Faber Book of Northern Legends* For the second time—but I hope not the last—I am indebted to Alan Howard for his striking illustrations and to Phyllis Hunt, most discerning and patient of editors, who has given me a great deal of help in shaping both anthologies. Although the number of authors, translators and books represented here is necessarily limited, the selection entailed working through a substantial amount of material; I have attempted to read, or at least skim, whatever North-west European folk-tales are available in English and I am most grateful to the staffs of the British Library and the London Library for having made the exercise so straightforward and enjoyable.

The Pleiades

Denmark

There was once a man and he had six sons. He did not give them, however, any names such as other people have, but called them according to their age, the Oldest, Next to the Oldest, the Next to the Next to the Oldest, the Next to the Next to the Youngest, the Next to the Youngest and the Youngest. They had no other names.

When the Oldest was eighteen and the Youngest twelve, their father sent them out into the world that each might learn a trade. They went together for a short distance until they came to a place where six roads diverged; there they separated and each was to go his own way. But before parting they agreed to meet in two years at that same place and to return to their father together.

On the day appointed they all met and went home to their father who asked each one what he had learned. The Oldest said that he was a ship-builder and could build ships which could propel themselves. The Next to the Oldest had gone to sea and had become a helmsman and could steer a ship over land as well as over water. The Next to the Next to the Oldest had only learned to listen, but that he could do so well that when he was in one country he could hear what was going on in another. The Next to the Next to the Youngest had become a sharpshooter, and he never missed his aim. The Next to the Youngest had learned how to climb, and he could climb up a wall like a fly and no cliff was too steep for him to scale.

When the father had heard what the five brothers could do, he said that it was all very well but that he had expected something more from them. Then he asked what the Youngest had learned; he had great hopes in him for he was his favourite. The Youngest was glad that it was at last his turn to speak, and he answered joyously that he had become a master-thief. When his father heard that, he was furious and exclaimed, "Shame on you, for the disgrace that you have brought upon me and the whole family."

Now it happened that at this very time the king's beautiful young daughter had been stolen by a wicked wizard, and the king promised the half of his realm and the princess in marriage to the one who should free her from the wizard. When the six brothers heard this they resolved to try their luck. The shipbuilder built a ship that went of itself. The helmsman steered it over land and sea. The listener listened carefully and at last said that he heard the wizard inside a mountain of glass. Thither they sailed. The climber quickly climbed to the top of the mountain and saw the ugly wizard lying sleeping with his head in the lap of the princess. Then he hurried down, and taking the little master-thief on his back, went into the inside of the mountain. The thief stole the princess so cleverly from under the head of the wizard that he did not notice it, but continued to sleep.

As soon as they were on board, the ship sailed away, but the listener had to continue to keep a watch on the wizard. When they were not far from land he said to the others: "Now the wizard is awaking! now he is stretching himself! now he misses the princess! now he is coming!"

Now the king's daughter was beside herself with fear, and declared that they would all die if there were not a sharpshooter on board. The wizard could fly through the air and would soon overtake them; he was also invulnerable except in one small black spot, not larger than a pinhead, in the middle of his chest. Hardly had she finished speaking when they saw the wizard in the distance rushing through the air. The sharpshooter took careful aim, shot, and his bullet struck the little black spot and at once the wizard burst into thousands of fiery pieces, and these we know as meteorites.

At last the six brothers reached home with the princess and brought her to the king. But they were all in love with her, and each one could truthfully say that without his help she could not have been saved. Then the king was distressed, for he did not know to whom he should give his daughter. And the princess was also sad, for she did not know whom she loved best.

But God would not that there should be strife among them, so he sent death to the six brothers and to the king's daughter in one and the same night. Then he made of the seven a constellation which men call the Pleiades. And of these stars the brightest is the princess and the faintest the little master-thief.

collected by SVEND GRUNDTVIG
translated by J. Grant Cramer

How Some Wild Animals Became Tame Ones

Lapland

Once upon a time there lived a miller who was so rich that, when he was going to be married, he asked to the feast not only his own friends but also the wild animals who dwelt in the hills and woods round about. The chief of the bears, the wolves, the foxes, the horses, the cows, the goats, the sheep, and the reindeer, all received invitations; and as they were not accustomed to weddings they were greatly pleased and flattered, and sent back messages in the politest language that they would certainly be there.

The first to start on the morning of the wedding-day was the bear, who always liked to be punctual; and, besides, he had a long way to go, and his hair, being so thick and rough, needed a good brushing before it was fit to be seen at a party. However, he took care to awaken very early, and set off down the road with a light heart. Before he had walked very far he met a boy who came whistling along, hitting at the tops of the flowers with a stick.

"Where are you going?" said he, looking at the bear in surprise, for he was an old acquaintance, and not generally so smart.

"Oh, just to the miller's marriage," answered the bear carelessly. "Of course, I would much rather stay at home, but the miller was so anxious I should be there that I really could not refuse."

"Don't go, don't go!" cried the boy. "If you do you will never come back! You have got the most beautiful skin in the world—just the kind that everyone is wanting, and they will be sure to kill you and strip you of it."

"I had not thought of that," said the bear, whose face turned white, only nobody could see it. "If you are certain that they would be so wicked—but perhaps you are jealous because nobody has invited *you*?"

"Oh, nonsense!" replied the boy angrily, "do as you see. It is your skin, and not mine; *I* don't care what becomes of it!" And he walked quickly on with his head in the air.

The bear waited until he was out of sight, and then followed him slowly, for he felt in his heart that the boy's advice was good, though he was too proud to say so.

The boy soon grew tired of walking along the road, and turned off into the woods, where there were bushes he could jump and streams he could wade; but he had not gone far before he met the wolf.

"Where are you going?" asked he, for it was not the first time he had seen him.

"Oh, just to the miller's marriage," answered the wolf, as the bear had done before him. "It is rather tiresome, of course—weddings are always so stupid; but still one must be good-natured!"

"Don't go!" said the boy again. "Your skin is so thick and warm, and winter is not far off now. They will kill you, and strip it from you."

The wolf's jaw dropped in astonishment and terror. "Do you *really* think that would happen?" he gasped.

"Yes, to be sure, I do," answered the boy. "But it is your affair, not mine. So good-morning," and on he went. The wolf stood still for a few minutes, for he was trembling all over, and then crept quietly back to his cave.

Next the boy met the fox, whose lovely coat of silvery grey was shining in the sun.

"You look very fine!" said the boy, stopping to admire him. "Are you going to the miller's wedding too?"

"Yes," answered the fox; "it is a long journey to take for such a thing as that, but you know what the miller's friends are like—so dull and heavy! It is only kind to go and amuse them a little."

"You poor fellow," said the boy pityingly. "Take my advice and stay at home. If you once enter the miller's gate his dogs will tear you in pieces."

"Ah, well, such things *have* occurred, I know," replied the fox gravely. And without saying any more he trotted off the way he had come.

His tail had scarcely disappeared, when a great noise of crashing branches was heard, and up bounded the horse, his black skin glistening like satin.

"Good morning," he called to the boy as he galloped past, "I can't

wait to talk to you now. I have promised the miller to be present at his
wedding-feast, and they won't sit down till I come."

"Stop! stop!" cried the boy after him, and there was something in
his voice that made the horse pull up. "What is the matter?" asked
he.

"You don't know what you are doing," said the boy. "If once you
go there you will never gallop through these woods any more. You
are stronger than many men, but they will catch you and put ropes
round you, and you will have to work and to serve them all the days of
your life."

The horse threw back his head at these words, and laughed scorn-
fully.

"Yes, I am stronger than many men," answered he, "and all the
ropes in the world would not hold me. Let them bind me as fast as
they will, I can always break loose, and return to the forest and
freedom."

And with this proud speech he gave a whisk of his long tail, and
galloped away faster than before.

But when he reached the miller's house everything happened as
the boy had said. While he was looking at the guests and thinking
how much handsomer and stronger he was than any of them, a rope
was suddenly flung over his head, and he was thrown down and a bit
thrust between his teeth. Then, in spite of his struggles, he was
dragged to a stable, and shut up for several days without any food, till
his spirit was broken and his coat had lost its gloss. After that he was
harnessed to a plough, and had plenty of time to remember all he had
lost through not listening to the counsel of the boy.

When the horse had turned a deaf ear to his words the boy
wandered idly along, sometimes gathering wild strawberries from a
bank, and sometimes plucking wild cherries from a tree, till he
reached a clearing in the middle of the forest. Crossing this open
space was a beautiful milk-white cow with a wreath of flowers round
her neck.

"Good-morning," she said pleasantly, as she came up to the place
where the boy was standing.

"Good-morning," he returned. "Where are you going in such a
hurry?"

"To the miller's wedding; I am rather late already, for the wreath
took such a long time to make, so I can't stop."

"Don't go," said the boy earnestly; "when once they have tasted
your milk they will never let you leave them, and you will have to
serve them all the days of your life."

"Oh, nonsense; what do *you* know about it?" answered the cow, who always thought she was wiser than other people. "Why, I can run twice as fast as any of them! I should like to see anybody try to keep me against my will." And, without even a polite bow, she went on her way, feeling very much offended.

But everything turned out just as the boy had said. The company had all heard of the fame of the cow's milk, and persuaded her to give them some, and then her doom was sealed. A crowd gathered round her, and held her horns so that she could not use them, and, like the horse, she was shut in the stable, and only let out in the mornings, when a long rope was tied round her head, and she was fastened to a stake in a grassy meadow.

And so it happened to the goat and to the sheep.

Last of all came the reindeer, looking as he always did, as if some serious business was on hand.

"Where are you going?" asked the boy, who by this time was tired of wild cherries, and was thinking of his dinner.

"I am invited to the wedding," answered the reindeer, "and the miller has begged me on no account to fail him."

"O fool!" cried the boy. "Have you no sense at all? Don't you know that when you get there they will hold you fast, for neither beast nor bird is as strong or as swift as you?"

"That is exactly why I am quite safe," replied the reindeer. "I am so strong that no one can bind me, and so swift that not even an arrow can catch me. So, goodbye for the present, you will soon see me back."

But none of the animals that went to the miller's wedding ever came back. And because they were self-willed and conceited, and would not listen to good advice, they and their children have been the servants of men to this very day.

retold by ANDREW LANG

The Three Heads of the Well
England

Long before Arthur and the Knights of the Round Table, there reigned in the eastern part of England a king who kept his court at Colchester. He was witty, strong, and valiant, by which means he subdued his enemies abroad, and secured peace among his subjects at home. Nevertheless, in the midst of his glory, his queen died, leaving behind her an only daughter, about fifteen years of age. This lady, from her courtly carriage, beauty and affability, was the wonder of all that knew her; but, as covetousness is said to be the root of all evil, so it happened in this instance. The king, hearing of a lady who had likewise an only daughter, for the sake of her riches had a mind to marry; though she was old, ugly, hooked-nosed, and hump-backed, yet all this could not deter him from marrying her. Her daughter, also, was a yellow dowdy, full of envy and ill-nature; and, in short, was much of the same mould as her mother. This signified nothing, for in a few weeks the king, attended by the nobility and gentry, brought his intended bride to his palace, where the marriage rites were performed. They had not been long in the court before they set the king against his own beautiful daughter, which was done by false reports and accusations. The young princess, having lost her father's love, grew weary of the court, and one day meeting with her father in the garden, she desired him, with tears in her eyes, to give her a small subsistence, and she would go and seek her fortune; to which the king consented, and ordered her mother-in-law to make up a small sum according to her discretion. She went to the queen, who gave her a canvas bag of brown bread and hard cheese, with a bottle of beer. Though this was but a very pitiful dowry for a king's daughter, she took it, returned thanks, and proceeded on her journey, passing through groves, woods, and valleys, till at length she saw an old man sitting on a stone at the mouth of a cave, who said, "Good morrow, fair maiden, whither away so fast?" "Aged father," says she, "I am going to seek my fortune." "What hast thou in thy bag and bottle?" "In my bag I have got bread and cheese, and in my bottle good small beer; will you please to partake of either?" "Yes," said he, "with all my heart." With that the lady pulled out her provisions, and bid him eat and welcome. He did so, and gave her many thanks, saying thus: "There is a thick thorny hedge before you, which will appear impassable; but take this wand in your hand, strike three times, and say, 'Pray, hedge, let me come through,' and it will open immediately; then, a little farther, you will find a well; sit down on the brink of it, and there will come up three golden heads, which will speak: pray do whatever they require." Promising she would follow his directions, she took her leave of him. Arriving at the hedge, and pursuing the old man's directions, it divided, and gave her a passage: then, going to the well, she had no sooner sat down than a golden head came up singing—

> *Wash me, and comb me,*
> *And lay me down softly,*
> *And lay me on a bank to dry,*
> *That I may look pretty*
> *When somebody comes by.*

"Yes," said she, and putting forth her hand, with a silver comb performed the office, placing it upon a primrose bank. Then came up a second and a third head, making the same request, which she complied with. She then pulled out her provisions and ate her dinner. Then said the heads one to another, "What shall we do for this lady who hath used us so kindly?" The first said, "I will cause such addition to her beauty as shall charm the most powerful prince in the world." The second said, "I will endow her with such perfume, both in body and breath, as shall far exceed the sweetest flowers." The third said, "My gift shall be none of the least, for, as she is a king's daughter, I'll make her so fortunate that she shall become queen to the greatest prince that reigns." This done, at their request she let them down into the well again, and so proceeded on her journey. She had not travelled long before she saw a king hunting in the park with his nobles; she would have avoided him, but the king having caught a sight of her, approached, and what with her beauty and perfumed breath, was so powerfully smitten, that he was not able to subdue his passion, but commenced his courtship immediately, and was so successful that he gained her love, and, conducting her to

his palace, he caused her to be clothed in the most magnificent manner.

This being ended, and the king finding that she was the King of Colchester's daughter, he ordered some chariots to be got ready, that he might pay the king a visit. The chariot in which the king and queen rode was adorned with rich ornamental gems of gold. The king, her father, was at first astonished that his daughter had been so fortunate as she was, till the young king made him sensible of all that happened. Great was the joy at court amongst all, with the exception of the queen and her club-footed daughter, who were ready to burst with malice, and envied her happiness; and the greater was their madness because she was now above them all. Great rejoicings, with feasting and dancing, continued many days. Then at length, with the dowry her father gave her, they returned home.

The deformed daughter, perceiving that her sister had been so happy in seeking her fortune, would needs do the same; so disclosing her mind to her mother, all preparations were made, and she was furnished not only with rich apparel, but sweetmeats, sugar, almonds, &c., in great quantities, and a large bottle of Malaga sack. Thus provided, she went the same road as her sister, and coming near the cave, the old man said, "Young woman whither so fast?" "What is that to you?" said she. "Then," said he, "what have you in your bag and bottle?" She answered, "Good things, which you shall not be troubled with." "Won't you give me some?" said he. "No, not a bit, nor a drop, unless it would choke you." The old man frowned, saying, "Evil fortune attend thee." Going on, she came to the hedge, through which she espied a gap, and thought to pass through it, but, going in, the hedge closed, and the thorns ran into her flesh, so that it was with great difficulty that she got out. Being now in a painful condition, she searched for water to wash herself, and, looking round, she saw the well; she sat down on the brink of it, and one of the heads came up, saying, "Wash me, comb me, and lay me down softly, &c." but she banged it with her bottle, saying, "Take this for your washing." So the second and third heads came up, and met with no better treatment than the first; whereupon the heads consulted among themselves what evils to plague her with for such usage. The first said, "Let her be struck with leprosy in her face." The second, "Let an additional smell be added to her breath." The third bestowed on her a husband, though but a poor country cobbler. This done she goes on till she came to a town, and it being market day, the people looked at her, and seeing such an evil face, fled out of her sight, all but a poor country cobbler (who not long before had mended the shoes of an old hermit, who having no money, gave him a box of ointment for the cure of the leprosy, and a bottle of spirits for a bad breath). Now the cobbler having a mind to do an act of charity, was induced to go up to her and ask her who she was. "I am," said she "the King of Colchester's daughter-in-law." "Well," said the cobbler, "if I restore you to your natural complexion, and make a sound cure both in face and breath, will you in reward take me for a husband?" "Yes, friend," replied she, "with all my heart." With this the cobbler applied the remedies, and they worked the effect in a few weeks, and then they were married, and after a few days they set forward for the court of Colchester. When the queen understood she had married a poor cobbler, she fell into distraction, and hanged herself for vexation. The death of the queen was not a source of sorrow to the king, who had only married her for her fortune, and bore her no affection; and shortly afterwards he gave the cobbler £100 to take the daughter to a remote part of the kingdom, where he lived many years mending shoes, while his wife assisted the house-keeping by spinning, and selling the results of her labour at the country market.

retold by JAMES ORCHARD HALLIWELL

Why the Sea is Salt

Norway

Once on a time, but it was a long, long time ago, there were two brothers, one rich and one poor. Now, one Christmas eve, the poor one hadn't so much as a crumb in the house, either of meat or bread, so he went to his brother to ask him for something to keep Christmas with, in God's name. It was not the first time his brother had been forced to help him, and you may fancy he wasn't very glad to see his face, but he said—

"If you will do what I ask you to do, I'll give you a whole flitch of bacon."

So the poor brother said he would do anything, and was full of thanks.

"Well, here is the flitch," said the rich brother, "and now go straight to Hell."

"What I have given my word to do, I must stick to," said the other; so he took the flitch and set off. He walked the whole day, and at dusk he came to a place where he saw a very bright light.

"Maybe this is the place," said the man to himself. So he turned aside, and the first thing he saw was an old, old man, with a long white beard, who stood in an outhouse, hewing wood for the Christmas fire.

"Good even," said the man with the flitch.

"The same to you; whither are you going so late?" said the man.

"Oh! I'm going to Hell, if I only knew the right way," answered the poor man.

"Well, you're not far wrong, for this is Hell," said the old man; "when you get inside they will be all for buying your flitch, for meat is scarce in Hell; but mind you don't sell it unless you get the hand-quern which stands behind the door for it. When you come out, I'll teach you how to handle the quern, for it's good to grind almost anything."

So the man with the flitch thanked the other for his good advice, and gave a great knock at the Devil's door.

When he got in, everything went just as the old man had said. All the devils, great and small, came swarming up to him like ants round an anthill, and each tried to outbid the other for the flitch.

"Well!" said the man, "by rights my old dame and I ought to have this flitch for our Christmas dinner; but since you have all set your hearts on it, I suppose I must give it up to you; but if I sell it at all, I'll have for it that quern behind the door yonder."

At first the Devil wouldn't hear of such a bargain, and chaffered and haggled with the man; but he stuck to what he said, and at last the Devil had to part with his quern. When the man got out into the yard, he asked the old woodcutter how he was to handle the quern; and after he had learned how to use it, he thanked the old man and went off home as fast as he could, but still the clock had struck twelve on Christmas eve before he reached his own door.

"Wherever in the world have you been?" said his old dame; "here have I sat hour after hour waiting and watching, without so much as two sticks to lay together under the Christmas brose."

"Oh!" said the man, "I couldn't get back before, for I had to go a long way first for one thing, and then for another; but now you shall see what you shall see."

So he put the quern on the table, and bade it first of all grind lights, then a table-cloth, then meat, then ale, and so on till they had got everything that was nice for Christmas fare. He had only to speak the word, and the quern ground out what he wanted. The old dame stood by blessing her stars, and kept on asking where he had got this wonderful quern, but he wouldn't tell her.

"It's all one where I got it from; you see the quern is a good one, and the mill-stream never freezes, that's enough."

So he ground meat and drink and dainties enough to last out till Twelfth Day, and on the third day he asked all his friends and kin to his house, and gave a great feast. Now, when his rich brother saw all that was on the table, and all that was behind in the larder, he grew quite spiteful and wild, for he couldn't bear that his brother should have anything.

"'Twas only on Christmas eve," he said to the rest, "he was in such straits, that he came and asked for a morsel of food in God's name, and now he gives a feast as if he were count or king"; and he turned to his brother and said—

"But whence, in Hell's name, have you got all this wealth?"

"From behind the door," answered the owner of the quern, for he didn't care to let the cat out of the bag. But later in the evening, when he had got a drop too much, he could keep his secret no longer, and brought out the quern and said—

"There, you see what has gotten me all this wealth"; and so he made the quern grind all kind of things. When his brother saw it, he set his heart on having the quern, and, after a deal of coaxing, he got it; but he had to pay three hundred dollars for it, and his brother bargained to keep it till hay-harvest, for he thought, if I keep it till then, I can make it grind meat and drink that will last for years. So you may fancy the quern didn't grow rusty for want of work, and when hay-harvest came, the rich brother got it, but the other took care not to teach him how to handle it.

It was evening when the rich brother got the quern home, and next morning he told his wife to go out into the hay-field and toss, while the mowers cut the grass, and he would stay at home and get the dinner ready. So, when dinner-time drew near, he put the quern on the kitchen table and said—

"Grind herrings and broth, and grind them good and fast."

So the quern began to grind herrings and broth; first of all, all the dishes full, then all the tubs full, and so on till the kitchen floor was quite covered. Then the man twisted and twirled at the quern to get it to stop, but for all his twisting and fingering the quern went on grinding, and in a little while the broth rose so high that the man was like to drown. So he threw open the kitchen door and ran into the parlour, but it wasn't long before the quern had ground the parlour full too, and it was only at the risk of his life that the man could get hold of the latch of the house door through the stream of broth. When he got the door open, he ran out and set off down the road, with the stream of herrings and broth at his heels, roaring like a waterfall over the whole farm.

Now, his old dame, who was in the field tossing hay, thought it a long time to dinner, and at last she said—

"Well! though the master doesn't call us home, we may as well go. Maybe he finds it hard work to boil the broth, and will be glad of my help."

The men were willing enough, so they sauntered homewards; but just as they had got a little way up the hill, what should they meet but herrings, and broth, and bread, all running and dashing, and splashing together in a stream, and the master himself running before them for his life, and as he passed them he bawled out—"Would to heaven each of you had a hundred throats! but take care you're not drowned in the broth."

Away he went, as though the Evil One were at his heels, to his brother's house, and begged him for God's sake to take back the quern that instant; for, said he—

"If it grinds only one hour more, the whole parish will be swallowed up by herrings and broth."

But his brother wouldn't hear of taking it back till the other paid him down three hundred dollars more.

So the poor brother got both the money and the quern, and it wasn't long before he set up a farm-house far finer than the one in which his brother lived, and with the quern he ground so much gold that he covered it with plates of gold; and as the farm lay by the sea-side, the golden house gleamed and glistened far away over the sea. All who sailed by put ashore to see the rich man in the golden house, and to see the wonderful quern, the fame of which spread far and wide, till there was nobody who hadn't heard tell of it.

So one day there came a skipper who wanted to see the quern; and the first thing he asked was if it could grind salt.

"Grind salt!" said the owner; "I should just think it could. It can grind anything."

When the skipper heard that, he said he must have the quern, cost what it would; for if he only had it, he thought he should be rid of his long voyages across stormy seas for a lading of salt. Well, at first the man wouldn't hear of parting with the quern; but the skipper begged and prayed so hard, that at last he let him have it, but he had to pay many, many thousand dollars for it. Now, when the skipper had got the quern on his back, he soon made off with it, for he was afraid lest the man should change his mind; so he had no time to ask how to handle the quern, but got on board his ship as fast as he could, and set sail. When he had sailed a good way off, he brought the quern on deck and said—

"Grind salt, and grind both good and fast."

Well, the quern began to grind salt so that it poured out like water; and when the skipper had got the ship full, he wished to stop the quern, but whichever way he turned it, and however much he tried, it was no good; the quern kept grinding on, and the heap of salt grew higher and higher, and at last down sunk the ship.

There lies the quern at the bottom of the sea, and grinds away at this very day, and that's why the sea is salt.

collected by PETER CHRISTEN ASBJÖRNEN and JÖRGEN I. MOE
translated by Sir George Webbe Dasent

The Bremen Town Musicians

Germany

A donkey had for years faithfully carried his master's sacks of wheat to the mill for grinding. But the donkey was losing his strength and was able to work less and less. His owner had about decided the animal was no longer worth his keep when the donkey, realizing that no kind wind was blowing in his direction, ran away. He took the road to Bremen. Once there, he thought, he would become a town musician. After travelling a while, he came upon a hunting dog lying by the roadside. The dog lay there panting and exhausted as if he had run a great distance.

"What makes you pant so, Catcher?" asked the donkey.

"Oh," said the dog, "I am old and getting weaker each day, and because I can no longer serve my master in the hunt, he wanted to beat me to death, so I've run away. But I don't know how I'm going to earn my bread."

"I'll tell you what to do," replied the donkey. "I'm on my way to Bremen to become a town musician. Come along and you can get a job too. I'll play the lute and you can try the kettle drums."

The dog was delighted and they continued on together. It was not long before they met a cat on the road who looked as mournful as three days of steady rain.

"What crossed your path, Old Whiskerwasher?" inquired the donkey.

"How can I be happy when I've had it up to my ears? I'm getting on in years and my teeth have gone dull. I'd rather sit behind the stove and dream than chase mice and so my mistress wanted to drown me. Well, I managed to get away, but good rat is expensive, and where shall I go?"

"Come with us to Bremen. You know all about night music and you, too, can get a job as a town musician."

The cat thought this a good idea and joined them.

The three fugitives soon came to a farm, where they saw a cock sitting on a gatepost screaming away at the top of his lungs.

"You'll burst our eardrums," the donkey said to the cock. "What's the matter?"

"Here I promised good weather for the holy day because it is the day Our Dear Lady washed the Christ child's shirts and wanted them to dry. But my mistress has no pity on me. Tomorrow is Sunday and guests are coming, and she has told the cook that she wants me in the soup. I'm to have my head chopped off this very evening. That's why I'm screaming as loud and as long as I still can."

"Nonsense," said the donkey. "Come with us. We're off to Bremen. You can find something better to do anywhere than die. You have a good voice, and with your help, if we all make music together, it will surely have style."

The cock agreed to this proposal and the four continued on their way.

Bremen was too far to reach in one day. By evening they had arrived at a forest and decided to spend the night there. The donkey and the dog lay down beneath a huge tree. The cat and the cock, however, made for the branches—the cock flying all the way to the top, where he felt himself safest. But before he went to sleep, he looked about in all directions, and it seemed to him he saw a light in the distance. He called down to his comrades that there must be a house not too far away.

"In that case," said the donkey, "let's get up and go there. The shelter here is pretty flimsy." And since it occurred to the dog that a few bones and a piece of meat would do him good, they all made their way in the direction of the light, which grew brighter and bigger, until they stood before a well-lighted thieves' hideout.

The donkey, as the tallest, went to the window and peered inside.

"What do you see, Greyhorse?" asked the cock.

"What I see," replied the donkey, "is a table loaded with lovely food and drink. And the thieves are sitting around it, enjoying themselves."

"That would be something for us," said the cock.

"Yes, indeed. If only we were inside," said the donkey.

The animals held a conference on how to get the thieves out of the house, and at last worked out a plan. The donkey was to stand on his hind legs with his forelegs on the window sill. The dog was to jump up on the donkey's back, the cat was to climb up on top of the dog, and last of all, the cock was to fly up and seat himself on the cat's head. When they were in position, the signal was given and they began to make music together: the donkey brayed, the dog howled, the cat meowed, the cock crowed. Then they broke through the window and into the room to the accompaniment of crashing glass.

The thieves jumped for fright at the unbearable noise and, convinced that the animals were ghosts, fled into the forest in terror.

The four comrades sat down at the table. They weren't choosy about leftovers and ate everything in sight as if they hadn't touched food in a month. When they had eaten their fill, they put out the lights and each, according to his nature and convenience, found himself a place to sleep.

The donkey lay down on the dung heap, the dog behind the door, the cat on the hearth near the warm ashes, and the cock settled himself on a rafter. And because they were tired out from their long hike, they soon fell asleep.

When midnight had passed, and the thieves saw from a distance that there were no longer any lights on in the house and that all seemed quiet, their chief said, "We shouldn't let them scare us out of our wits."

He ordered one of his men to go back to the house and look around. The messenger, finding all quiet, went into the kitchen to get a light. He mistook the cat's glowing eyes for live coals and struck a match on them. This was no joke to the cat, who sprang at his face, spitting and scratching.

The terrified thief tried to get out the back door, but the dog, who lay there, sprang up and bit him in the leg. As he ran by the dung heap in the yard, the donkey landed him a neat blow with his hind legs; the cock on his roost, awakened by the noise, cried kikeriki.

The thief ran as fast as he could to his chief and said, "There is a terrible witch in the house. She attacked me and scratched my face with her long nails. At the door there is a man with a knife and he stuck me in the leg with it. In the yard there's a black monster, who beat me with a club; and on the roof there sat a judge who cried, 'Bring the scoundrels to me.'

"Then I got away."

After that the thieves never dared to come near the house, and the four Bremen town musicians felt themselves so much at home they decided to remain for good.

And this tale's still warm from the telling, for I've just heard it.

collected by JACOB and WILHELM GRIMM
translated by Elizabeth Shub

ᚻᚻ

The Wizards of the Vestmanna Isles
Iceland

ᚻᚻᚻᚻᚻᚻᚻᚻᚻᚻᚻᚻᚻᚻᚻᚻᚻᚻᚻᚻᚻᚻᚻᚻᚻᚻᚻᚻᚻᚻᚻᚻᚻᚻ ᚻᚻᚻᚻᚻᚻᚻᚻᚻᚻᚻᚻᚻ

When the Black Death was raging in Iceland, eighteen wizards gathered, swore friendship with one another, and sailed out to the Vestmanna Isles, intending to ward off death there as long as they could. As soon as they saw by their secret arts that the sickness was abating on the mainland, they wanted to find out whether anyone there was still alive; so they agreed to send one of their company to the mainland, and for this errand they chose one who was neither the most nor the least skilled in their arts. They ferried him to land, and told him that if he was not back before Christmas they would send him a Sending which would kill him. This was early in Advent.

The man went off, walked a long way, and wandered far and wide. But nowhere did he see a living soul; farms stood open, and dead bodies lay about, scattered here and there. Finally he came to one farm whose doors were shut. He was amazed, and now hope stirred in him that he might find some living man. He knocked, and out came a young and pretty girl. He greeted her, but she flung her arms round his neck and wept for joy to see a man, for she said she had thought there was nobody left alive but her. She asked him to stay with her, and he agreed. So now they went indoors and talked; she asked him where he had come from, and where he was going. He told her, and also told her that he would have to be back before Christmas, but all the same she asked him to stay with her as long as he could, and he was so sorry for her that he promised that he would. She told him there was nobody alive in those parts, for she said she had walked a whole week's journey from her house in each direction, and found no one.

Now time slipped by and Christmas drew near, and then the man from the islands wanted to go. The girl begged him to stay, and said that his friends would not be so hard-hearted as to make him pay for

it if he stayed with her when she was left all alone in the world. So he
let himself be persuaded.

And now Christmas Eve had come, and now he is determined to
go, whatever she may say. So then she sees that it's no good pleading
any longer, and says: "Do you really think you can get out to the
islands tonight? Don't you think you might just as well die here
beside me as die somewhere on the way?"

The man realized that the time was too short now, and resigned
himself to stay quietly there and wait for death where he was. So the
night passed, and he was very gloomy, but the girl was as merry as
could be, and asked whether he could see how the men on the Isles
were getting on. He said that they were preparing to send a Sending
ashore, and that it would arrive that day. Now the girl sat down on
the bed beside him, while he lay in bed, a little way behind her. He
said that he was beginning to grow sleepy, and that this was due to the
Sending's onslaught. Then he fell asleep. The girl sat at the foot of
the bed, and she would constantly rouse him a little and make him
tell her where the Sending now was. But the nearer it came the deeper
he slept, and finally, just after saying that the Sending had reached
her farm-lands, he fell into such a deep sleep that she could not wake
him again—nor was it long before she saw a russet vapour come into
the farmhouse.

This vapour glided gently, very gently, up the room towards her,
and then took on human shape. The girl asks the Sending where it is
going, and it tells her what its errand is, and tells her to get up off the
bed—"for I can't get at him on account of you," it says.

The girl says that in that case it will have to do something for her.
The Sending asks what that might be. The girl says it is to let her see
how huge it could make itself. The Sending agrees to this, and now it
grows so huge that it fills the whole house.

Then the girl says: "Now I want to see how small you can make
yourself."

The Sending says it can turn itself into a fly, and with this it
changes to the likeness of a fly, for it imagines that now it will be able
to slip under the girl's arm and get at the man in bed. But it settles on
a marrowbone which the girl was holding and crawls right into it, and
the girl sticks a plug in the hole. Then she puts the bone in her pocket
with the Sending inside it, and now she wakes the man.

He woke up at once, and was much amazed at being still alive.
Then the girl asks him where the Sending is now, and he says he has
no idea what has become of it. Then the girl says she had long
suspected that those fellows out on the Isles were no great wizards. So

now the man was very glad, and they both enjoyed Christmas and were quite contented.

But when New Year drew near, the man began to be silent, and the girl asks what the matter is. He says that the men of the Isles are now busy preparing another Sending, "and they are all of them putting strength into it. It is to come here on New Year's Eve, and there's nothing that can save me then."

The girl said she would not cross that bridge before she came to it— "and you ought not to be afraid of Sendings from those men in the Isles."

She was as merry as could be, so he felt ashamed of showing any weakness.

On New Year's Eve he says the Sending has come ashore— "and it is advancing rapidly, for great strength has been put into it."

The girl tells him to come out with her; he does so, and they walk till they come to a thicket. There she halts, and pulls some branches aside, and there in front of them is a slab of rock. The girl lifts the slab, and there underneath it is an underground chamber. They both go down into it, and a gloomy, ghastly place it is; there is one dim lamp, and it is burning human belly-fat in a human skull. In a bed near this lamp lies an old man, rather ghastly-looking; his eyes are blood-red, and all in all he is horrible enough for the man from the Isles to be quite impressed.

"Well, foster-daughter," says the old man, "there must be something new going on if you are out and about. It's a long while since I saw you. What can I do for you now?"

Then the girl tells him everything that had happened to her, and all about the man, and about the first Sending. The old man asks her to let him see the bone. She does, and he seemed to turn into quite a different person as soon as he was holding it; he turned it round and round in all directions, and stroked it all over.

Then the girl says: "Be quick and help me, foster-father, because my man is beginning to feel sleepy now, and that's a sign that the Sending will soon be here."

The old man takes the plug out of the bone, and out comes the fly. He strokes and pats the fly, and says: "Off you go now, and go to meet any Sendings from the Isles and swallow them up."

Then there was a mighty crash, and the fly zoomed off, and it had grown so huge that one jaw touched the sky and the other scraped the ground; in this way it met all Sendings that came from the Isles, and so the man was saved.

So home they went from the underground chamber, the girl and the man from the Vestmanna Isles, and they settled on her farm. They got married soon after, and increased and multiplied and filled the land. And that's as much as I know about this story.

collected by JÓN ÁRNASON
translated by Jacqueline Simpson

The Old Troll of Big Mountain
Sweden

Once there lived a poor crofter and his wife who had nothing more in this world than their little cottage, two goats, and a boy-child of five whose name was Olle.

The crofter and his wife worked far away from their cottage every day, so they had a paddock for the goats to graze in. They gave Olle a bread roll and a mug of milk, then they locked the door behind them and put the key under the doorstep.

One night when they came home, both goats were gone. Someone on the highway said he had seen the evil old troll of Big Mountain dragging them away.

You can imagine their distress! Now the crofter and his wife had even less to live on than before, and instead of goat's milk, Olle got nothing but water in his mug. But worst of all, no one could be sure that the evil old troll would not come back, put Olle in a sack, and carry him away up the mountain. The troll was known to have stolen children before, though no one knew what he did with them because none ever came back.

Every day before they left home, the crofter and his wife warned Olle never to sit by the window; for who could tell, the old troll might pass by and catch sight of the boy. If the troll ever knocked on the door, they told Olle, shout "Father, Father," exactly as if his father were at home, because that would surely scare the old troll and send him away.

So that Olle would recognize the troll, his parents described him carefully. He was terribly ugly, had real bushes for eyebrows, a mouth that reached from ear to ear, a nose as thick as a turnip, and instead of a left hand, a wolf's paw.

Yes, Olle would keep a lookout and defend himself, he promised them, and he began to make some weapons. He hammered a nail into a log and it became a lance. He ground an old knife, meant for splitting kindling, against a stone, and it became a sword. That old troll had better watch out, or he would be sorry.

One day as Olle was busy polishing his lance and his sword, he heard someone groping at the door. Olle looked out of the window and saw a man with a sack on his back crouching on his knees and poking his hand under the doorstep. It was none other than the evil old troll who had come to take Olle away, but Olle did not know it.

"What are you looking for?" asked Olle.

Of course, the troll was looking for the key so he could come and steal Olle, but naturally he did not want to say so. "I've lost a coin," he said instead. "It rolled right under your step. Will you come out and help me look for it?"

"No," said Olle. "Father and Mother have locked me in so that I will be safe from a wicked old troll."

The troll looked at Olle out of the corner of his eye. He wondered if the boy had any idea who he was. "Well, I don't look like an old troll, do I?" he said to test him.

"Oh, no. I'm not afraid of *you*. And I am not afraid of the old troll either, for if he comes here, he'll regret it. I have a lance and sword in here, you know. Look!"

The old troll peered through the windowpane, but pretended that he could not see anything. Then he asked Olle where the key was, so that he could unlock the door and come in and see better.

"Oh, yes," said Olle. "The key is under the first broken step on the right side."

Indeed, there it was. Quickly the old troll unlocked the door and stalked in. And to tell the truth, Olle was glad to have company. Proudly and eagerly he showed the old troll how finely he had ground his sword and what a wonderful lance a nail in a log makes. He was even rather wishing the old troll would come, so that he could pay him back for stealing their goats.

"I believe I know where he hides his goats," said the old troll. "If you come with me a little way into the woods, you might find them."

That was a good idea, thought Olle. Imagine, if he could bring home the stolen goats.

"Well, shall we go then?" said the troll.

"Yes," said Olle.

Olle wanted to bring along something to eat, because the troll's pastures were probably a long way off. So he broke his bread into pieces and put them in his pocket. He offered the old troll a piece, but the troll immediately said No. The reason for this was that trolls can never harm anyone from whom they have accepted something. If the troll took the bread now, he would not be able to stuff Olle into his sack. And that, of course, would never do.

When Olle was ready he reached for the old troll's hand, expecting to be led to where the goats were. But the troll pushed his hand away.

"You must take my right hand," said the troll. "I have hurt the left one." He showed Olle his left hand, which was bandaged with a thick cloth.

Olle felt sorry for him. "Oh, my. You poor man. Let me blow on it, that will make it better," he said.

But that didn't help. His only thought was to leave without being seen. It would have been quicker, of course, to stuff Olle into the sack right away, but as he was walking along so willingly, that saved the trouble of carrying him.

And so they walked hand in hand, Olle with his lance and sword ready under his arm, in case they met the evil old troll.

After they had gone a little way into the forest, Olle was tired and sat down on a stone. He began to eat his bread, for he was hungry, too.

The old troll eyed him. He wondered if this wasn't the moment to put the boy in the sack. Besides, it annoyed him that Olle was not afraid of him. That wasn't right. It would have been better to put him in the sack kicking and yelling the way all the other children did. And so he decided to scare Olle.

"Olle," he said, "suppose *I* were the old troll."

"Oh, no," Olle said, looking at him. "You don't look like him at all. He has bushes for eyebrows, and you haven't. He has a mouth that goes from ear to ear, and you haven't. And he has a wolf's paw instead of a left hand, and you haven't. So don't think you can fool me."

"How *do* I look, then?" asked the old troll.

"Like any other old man, of course," Olle reassured him.

That sounded so funny to the old troll's ears that he let out a loud guffaw. And in the same moment Olle threw a piece of bread into his open mouth.

"That's for being so good to me, not like an old troll at all."

"Oho, oho, oho," the old troll coughed with all his might. But however much he coughed, the bread did not come up; it slid farther and farther down his throat, until he swallowed it.

Now a strange thing happened. The old troll could not treat Olle the way he had intended to. Now that he had accepted something from Olle, he could not wish him ill.

"So you think I look like a man," said the troll. "It's the first time anybody ever said that to me. But if I look like a man, I had better act like one. Listen!"

He stood up and pulled a small pipe from his pocket and began to play it.

Olle listened. He thought he heard someone answering from the forest. Then the old troll blew once more, and again Olle pricked up his ears. Now he could hear footsteps, some light and some heavy, running across the twigs and moss.

The old troll blew one more time.

Something white appeared among the tree trunks, and Olle saw his parents' goats, Pearl and Flower, running towards him. They recognized him, and pushed and butted him. Olle was so excited that he shouted for sheer joy, and jumped from one leg to the other.

But there were more steps. Behind Pearl and Flower came hundreds of little kids, tripping out, tiny and delicate, just like tufts of white wool beside the bigger goats.

"But whose are these other goats?" asked Olle, looking at the old troll.

"Troll ways are different from man's ways, and goats have many kids when they stay with the old troll on Big Mountain," he replied, and patted Olle on the head. "But run along now. You must be home before your mother and father return."

Olle nodded, but before he had time to say a word, the troll had hurried in among the fir trees, because trolls do not like to be thanked.

Olle stood quite still for a moment, wondering where he had gone, but then he patted the goats again and they all set off for home.

On the way Olle met some people. They stopped, amazed at the sight of a small boy leading two goats and so many, many kids. They followed Olle to his cottage, and as the herd was let into the paddock, they stood gaping, a ring of wide eyes around the fence.

Just then Olle's father and mother arrived. When they saw their boy in the midst of all the goats, they were so surprised they had to sit down on a stone. Then Olle told his story and they wrung their hands and groaned. Who could have gathered all those goats? It sounded like magic. It couldn't have been the old troll, could it?

"No, it wasn't," said Olle. "He had big eyebrows, but they weren't real bushes. And he had a big mouth, too, but it didn't go from ear to ear. And he certainly didn't have a wolf's paw for a left hand. His left hand was all bandaged because he had hurt himself."

"Gracious!" exclaimed the crofter and his wife and all the others around the fence. "It *was* the old troll. He always wraps a cloth round his paw so as not to be recognized when he is passing the cottages."

Olle sat down and looked around at all the worried faces. He still could not understand. "Well then, maybe even bad old trolls are good sometimes," he said at last.

And no one who saw all those goats could doubt it, though no one there would ever have believed it before.

retold by ANNA WAHLENBERG
translated by Holger Lundbergh

Jorinde and Joringel

Germany

There was once an old castle right in the middle of a great, thick forest, and an old woman lived in it all alone; she was a witch. Every morning she changed herself into a cat or a screech-owl, every evening she changed back and looked like a decent human being. She knew how to entice wild animals and birds, and then she slaughtered them, boiled them and roasted them.

When anyone stepped within one hundred paces of the castle, his limbs were locked and he was unable to move an inch until the witch released him; and if a chaste young girl entered this circle, the witch turned her into a bird and stuffed her into a wickerwork cage and carried the cage into one of the castle chambers. She had all of seven thousand such cages, each with its own rare bird, in the castle.

Now there was once a young girl called Jorinde; she was more beautiful than anyone else at all. She and a handsome young man called Joringel had pledged themselves to one another. They were about to be married and were entirely wrapped up in each other. So that they could talk alone together for once in a while, they went walking in the forest.

"Beware!" said Joringel. "Don't go too close to the castle."

It was a lovely evening: the sun glanced between the tree trunks, shafts of light pierced the dark green of the forest, and the turtle-dove sang dolefully from the old hawthorn bushes.

Now and then Jorinde wept. She sat down in the sunlight and moaned; and Joringel moaned too. They felt so dismayed—as if they were about to die. They stared about them, and were lost, and did not know the way home. Half of the sun still stood above the mountain and half was below it.

Joringel peered through the undergrowth and saw the old walls of the castle only a few paces away. He was startled and scared to death.

Jorinde sang:

> *My little bird with the little ring red*
> *Sings Sorrow, Sorrow, Sorrow*
> *He sings the little dove will soon be dead,*
> *Sings Sorrow, Sorr . . . tsicuet, tsicuet, tsicuet.*

Joringel looked at Jorinde. Jorinde had been turned into a nightingale and sang "tsicuet, tsicuet". A screech-owl with glowing eyes flew round them three times and three times called "Tu-whit, Tu-whoo."

Joringel could not move; he stood there like a stone, he could not cry or speak or move hand or foot.

Now the sun had gone down. The owl flew into a bush and at once an old woman walked out of it, crooked and yellow and skinny: great red eyes, crooked nose so long that it touched her chin. She murmured, snared the nightingale, and carried it off on her hand.

Joringel was unable to say one word or move one step; the nightingale was gone.

After a long while the hag came back and said in a hollow voice: "Greetings, Zachiel! When the moon shines into the cage, let him loose, Zachiel, at the appointed hour!"

Then Joringel stood free. He fell on to his knees in front of the hag and begged her to give him back his Jorinde. But the witch replied that he would never see her again, and turned her back on him.

Joringel called out after her, he cried, he moaned, but all in vain. "Oh! What will become of me?" Joringel walked away and came at last to a remote village, and there he tended the sheep for a long time. He often walked round the castle but kept his distance from it.

Then one night Joringel dreamed that he found a blood-red flower with a fine large pearl in the middle of it. He picked the flower and went to the castle with it; whatever he touched with the flower was released from its enchantment; and he dreamed that he had won back his Jorinde with it.

As soon as he woke in the morning, Joringel began to search hill and dale for the flower of his dream; he searched for eight days and early on the morning of the ninth day he found the blood-red flower. A heavy dew-drop lay in the middle of it, as large as the finest of pearls.

Joringel carried this flower by day and night until he reached the

castle. When he stepped within one hundred paces of the castle, his limbs were not locked and he walked straight up to the gate.

Joringel rejoiced. He touched the gate with the flower and it sprang open. He walked through it, into the courtyard, listened, listened for the sound of birdsong; at last he heard it. He went and found the chamber where the witch was feeding the birds in the seven thousand cages.

When she saw Joringel she was angry, very angry; she yelled at him, she fumed and foamed, but she was unable to come within two paces of him.

Joringel took no notice, he went and checked the cages with the birds inside them. But there were many hundreds of nightingales. How would Joringel ever find his Jorinde again?

While he was busy with the cages, Joringel saw the old woman furtively pick up one cage with a bird in it and make for the door. He leaped across the chamber, and with the flower he touched the cage. He touched the hag too, and put an end to her magic powers.

And there stood Jorinde, her arms around his neck, as beautiful as she had been before. Then Joringel turned all the other birds back into young girls; and then he went home with his Jorinde, and they lived happily ever after.

collected by JACOB and WILHELM GRIMM
translated by Hildegund Kübler and Kevin Crossley-Holland

ᏏᏏ

A Stork is not always a Stork

Denmark

ᏏᏏ

Storks are storks, and men are men, and some say that's the end of it. But sometimes storks are men, and men are storks, and this story is the proof of it.

Not so very long ago, on a farm in Denmark, there was a man mowing a field of rye, and as his scythe went forward, a stork kept hopping beside him. This made him very nervous, for he feared he might get a good deep peck. "Be off with you!" he said, and, "Mind your own business, stork!" But it served no purpose, and at last he grew so rattled that he plucked out his short knife and flung it, *zip*, at the stork's head. Luckily he missed, it fell to the ground, and the stork picked it up and flew off.

Soon after this the man who had been mowing felt an urge to go travelling. Try as he would, he could not resist it, so he left the farm and signed for a sailor. Now he would be among icebergs and now off palm-treed coasts; to-day they would sail up steamy rivers, to-morrow down skerried creeks. Nor was he always on sea, for sometimes the urge drove him through jungles and deserts or over frozen plateaux. It was a cruel life he had of it, nor could he tell why. All he knew was that he had to keep going until somewhere, some time, he found something, he knew not what.

After many long years he found himself in Egypt, where he took lodging at an inn. The landlord asked him what he was doing so far from home. "If only I knew!" sighed the traveller, and went on to explain that he had never travelled farther than the nearest farm till after he flung his knife at a stork. "Since then," he said, "I have known not a single day's rest."

The landlord went out from the room, but in a moment or two he returned. "Would this be the knife?" he asked—and it was. "Yes," said the landlord, "and if it hadn't been that I brought up fourteen children on your father's barn, I should certainly have done you an injury that day."

As soon as the traveller received his knife again, he thought only of home. But first he had to meet the fourteen children, and bonny children they were too, without a feather among them at that moment. He took the next ship back to Denmark, where he told his story to all who would listen. But some said storks are storks, and men are men, and that's the end of it. But most agreed that storks are sometimes men, and men are storks, and reckoned this story the proof of it.

retold by GWYN JONES

ㅁㅁㅁ

Tom Tit Tot
England

ㅁㅁㅁ

Once upon a time there was a woman, and she baked five pies. And when they came out of the oven, they were that overbaked the crusts were too hard to eat. So she says to her daughter:

"Darter," says she, "put you them there pies on the shelf, and leave 'em there a little, and they'll come again."—She meant, you know, the crust would get soft.

But the girl, she says to herself: "Well, if they'll come again, I'll eat 'em now." And she set to work and ate 'em all, first and last.

Well, come supper-time the woman said: "Go you, and get one o' them there pies. I dare say they've come again now."

The girl went and she looked, and there was nothing but the dishes. So back she came and says she: "Noo, they ain't come again."

"Not one of 'em?" says the mother.

"Not one of 'em," says she.

"Well, come again, or not come again," said the woman, "I'll have one for supper."

"But you can't, if they ain't come," said the girl.

"But I can," says she. "Go you, and bring the best of 'em."

"Best or worst," says the girl, "I've ate 'em all, and you can't have one till that's come again."

Well, the woman she was done, and she took her spinning to the door to spin, and as she span she sang:

> *"My darter ha' ate five, five pies today.*
> *My darter ha' ate five, five pies today."*

The king was coming down the street, and he heard her sing, but what she sang he couldn't hear, so he stopped and said:

"What was that you were singing, my good woman?"

The woman was ashamed to let him hear what her daughter had been doing, so she sang, instead of that:

"My darter ha' spun five, five skeins today.
My darter ha' spun five, five skeins today."

"Stars o' mine!" said the king, "I never heard tell of anyone that could do that."

Then he said: "Look you here, I want a wife, and I'll marry your daughter. But look you here," says he, "eleven months out of the year she shall have all she likes to eat, and all the gowns she likes to get, and all the company she likes to keep; but the last month of the year she'll have to spin five skeins every day, and if she don't I shall kill her."

"All right," says the woman; for she thought what a grand marriage that was. And as for the five skeins, when the time came, there'd be plenty of ways of getting out of it, and likeliest, he'd have forgotten all about it.

Well, so they were married. And for eleven months the girl had all she liked to eat, and all the gowns she liked to get, and all the company she liked to keep.

But when the time was getting over, she began to think about the skeins and to wonder if he had 'em in mind. But not one word did he say about 'em, and she thought he'd wholly forgotten 'em.

However, the last day of the last month he takes her to a room she'd never set eyes on before. There was nothing in it but a spinning-wheel and a stool. And says he: "Now, my dear, here you'll be shut in tomorrow with some victuals and some flax, and if you haven't spun five skeins by the night, your head'll go off."

And away he went about his business.

Well, she was that frightened, she'd always been such a gatless girl, that she didn't so much as know how to spin, and what was she to do tomorrow with no one to come nigh her to help her? She sat down on a stool in the kitchen, and law! how she did cry!

However, all of a sudden she heard a sort of a knocking low down on the door. She upped and opened it, and what should she see but a small little black thing with a long tail. That looked up at her right curious, and that said:

"What are you a-crying for?"

"What's that to you?" says she.

"Never you mind," that said, "but tell me what you're a-crying for."

"That won't do me no good if I do," says she.

"You don't know that," that said, and twirled that's tail round.

"Well," says she, "that won't do no harm, if that don't do no good," and she upped and told about the pies, and the skeins, and everything.

"This is what I'll do," says the little black thing. "I'll come to your window every morning and take the flax and bring it spun at night."

"What's your pay?" says she.

That looked out of the corner of that's eyes, and that said: "I'll give you three guesses every night to guess my name, and if you haven't guessed it before the month's up you shall be mine."

Well, she thought, she'd be sure to guess that's name before the month was up. "All right," says she, "I agree."

"All right," that says, and law! how that twirled that's tail.

Well, the next day, her husband took her into the room, and there was the flax and the day's food.

"Now, there's the flax," says he, "and if that ain't spun up this night, off goes your head." And then he went out and locked the door.

He'd hardly gone, when there was a knocking against the window.

She upped and she oped it, and there sure enough was the little old thing sitting on the ledge.

"Where's the flax?" says he.

"Here it be," says she. And she gave it to him.

Well, come the evening a knocking came again to the window. She upped and she oped it, and there was the little old thing with five skeins of flax on his arm.

"Here it be," says he, and he gave it to her.

"Now, what's my name?" says he.

"What, is that Bill?" says she.

"Noo, that ain't," says he, and he twirled his tail.

"Is that Ned?" says she.

"Noo, that ain't," says he, and he twirled his tail.

"Well, is that Mark?" says she.

"Noo, that ain't," says he, and he twirled his tail harder, and away he flew.

Well, when her husband came in, there were the five skeins ready for him. "I see I shan't have to kill you tonight, my dear," says he; "You'll have your food and your flax in the morning," says he, and away he goes.

Well, every day the flax and the food were brought, and every day
that there little black impet used to come mornings and evenings.
And all the day the girl sate trying to think of names to say to it
when it came at night. But she never hit on the right one. And as
it got towards the end of the month, the impet began to look so
maliceful, and that twirled that's tail faster and faster each time she
gave a guess.

At last it came to the last day but one. The impet came at night
along with the five skeins, and that said:

"What, ain't you got my name yet?"

"Is that Nicodemus?" says she.

"Noo, 't ain't," that says.

"Is that Sammle?" says she.

"Noo, 't ain't," that says.

"A-well, is that Methusalem?" says she.

"Noo, 't ain't that neither," that says.

Then that looks at her with that's eyes like a coal of fire, and that
says: "Woman, there's only tomorrow night, and then you'll be
mine!" And away it flew.

Well, she felt that horrid. However, she heard the king coming
along the passage. In he came, and when he sees the five skeins, he
says, says he:

"Well, my dear," says he. "I don't see but what you'll have your
skeins ready tomorrow night as well, and as I reckon I shan't have to
kill you, I'll have supper in here tonight." So they brought supper,
and another stool for him, and down the two sate.

Well, he hadn't eaten but a mouthful or so, when he stops and
begins to laugh.

"What is it?" says she.

"A-why," says he, "I was out a-hunting today, and I got away to a
place in the wood I'd never seen before. And there was an old
chalk-pit. And I heard a kind of a sort of humming. So I got off my
hobby, and I went right quiet to the pit, and I looked down. Well,
what should there be but the funniest little black thing you ever set
eyes on. And what was that doing, but that had a little spinning-
wheel, and that was spinning wonderful fast, and twirling that's tail.
And as that span that sang:

> 'Nimmy nimmy not
> My name's Tom Tit Tot.'"

Well, when the girl heard this, she felt as if she could have jumped
out of her skin for joy, but she didn't say a word.

Next day that there little thing looked so maliceful when he came for the flax. And when night came she heard that knocking against the window panes. She opened the window, and that come right in on the ledge. That was grinning from ear to ear, and Oo! that's tail was twirling round so fast.

"What's my name?" that says, as that gave her the skeins.

"Is that Solomon?" she says, pretending to be afeard.

"Noo, 'tain't," that says, and that came farther into the room.

"Well, is that Zebedee?" says she again.

"Noo, 'tain't," says the impet. And then that laughed and twirled that's tail till you could hardly see it.

"Take time, woman," that says: "next guess, and you're mine." And that stretched out that's black hands at her.

Well, she backed a step or two, and she looked at it, and then she laughed out, and says she, pointing her finger at it:

> 'Nimmy nimmy not
> My name's Tom Tit Tot.'"

Well, when that heard her, that gave an awful shriek and away that flew into the dark, and she never saw it any more.

retold by JOSEPH JACOBS

Snipp, Snapp, Snorium

Sweden

᛭᛭᛭

There was once a miller who had three children, two girls and a boy. When the miller died, and the children divided the property, the daughters took the entire mill, and left their brother nothing but three sheep, that he tended in the forest. As he was one day wandering about, he met an old man, with whom he exchanged a sheep for a dog named *Snipp*; on the following day the same old man met him again, when he exchanged another sheep with him for a dog named *Snapp*; and on the third day his third sheep, for a dog named *Snorium*. The three dogs were large and strong, and obedient to their master in everything.

When the lad found there was no good to be done at home, he resolved to go out in the world and seek his fortune. After long wandering he came to a large city, in which the houses were hung with black, and everything betokened some great and universal calamity. The youth took up his quarters with an old fisherman, of whom he inquired the cause of this mourning. The fisherman informed him that there was a huge serpent named *Turenfax*, which inhabited an island out in the ocean; that every year a pure maiden must be given him to be devoured; and that the lot had now fallen on the king's only daughter. When the youth had heard this, he formed the resolution of venturing a contest with the serpent, and rescuing the princess, provided fortune would befriend him.

On the appointed day the youth sailed over to the island, and awaited whatever might happen. While he was sitting, he saw the young princess drawing near in a boat, accompanied by a number of

people. The king's daughter stopped at the foot of the mountain
and wept bitterly. The youth then approached her, greeted her
courteously, and comforted her to the best of his power. When a
short time had passed thus, he said: "Snipp! go to the mountain-
cave, and see whether the serpent is coming." But the dog returned,
wagged his tail, and said that the serpent had not yet made his
appearance. When some time had elapsed, the youth said: "Snapp!
go to the mountain-cave, and see whether the serpent is coming."
The dog went, but soon returned without having seen the serpent.
After a while the youth said: "Snorium! go to the mountain-cave, and
see whether the serpent is coming." The dog went, but soon returned
trembling violently. The youth could now easily guess that the
serpent was approaching, and, consequently, made himself ready for
the fight.

As Turenfax came hastening down the mountain, the youth set his
dogs Snipp and Snapp on him. A desperate battle then ensued; but
the serpent was so strong that the dogs were unable to master him.
When the youth observed this, he set on his third dog, Snorium, and
now the conflict became even fiercer; but the dogs got the mastery,
and the game did not end until Turenfax received his death-wound.

When the serpent was dead the king's daughter thanked her
deliverer with many affectionate expressions for her safety, and
besought him to accompany her to the royal palace. But the youth
would try his luck in the world for some time longer, and therefore
declined her invitation. It was, however, agreed on between them
that the youth should return in a year and woo the fair maiden. On
parting the princess brake her gold chain in three, and bound a
portion round the neck of each of the dogs. To the young man she
gave her ring, and they promised ever to be faithful to each other.

The young man now travelled about in the wide world, as we have
said, and the king's daughter returned home. On her way she was
met by a courtier, who forced her to make oath that he and no other
had slain Turenfax. This courtier was thenceforward looked upon as
a most doughty champion, and got a promise of the princess. But the
maiden would not break her faith to the youth, and deferred the
marriage from day to day.

When the year was expired, the youth returned from his wandering, and came to the great city. But now the houses were hung with
scarlet, and all things seemed to indicate a great and general rejoic-
ing. The youth again took up his quarters with the old fisherman, and
asked what might be the cause of all the joy. He was informed that a
courtier had killed Turenfax, and was now about to celebrate his

nuptials with the king's fair daughter. No one has heard what the miller's son said on receiving this intelligence; though it may easily be imagined that he was not greatly delighted at it.

When dinner-time came, the youth felt a longing to partake of the king's fare, and his host was at a great loss how this could be brought to pass. But the youth said: "Snipp! go up to the palace, and bring me a piece of game from the king's table. Fondle the young princess; but strike the false courtier a blow that he may not soon forget." Snipp did as his master had commanded him; he went up to the palace, caressed the fair princess, but struck the courtier a blow that made him black and blue; then, seizing a piece of game, he ran off. Hereupon there arose a great uproar in the hall, and all were filled with wonder, excepting the king's daughter; for she had recognised her gold neck-chain, and thence divined who the dog's master was.

The next day a similar scene was enacted. The youth was inclined to eat some pastry from the king's own table, and the fisherman was at a loss how this could be brought about. But the youth said: "Snapp! go up to the palace, and bring me some pastry from the king's table. Fondle the young princess; but strike the false courtier a blow that he may not soon forget." Snapp did as his master had commanded him; he went up to the palace, broke through the sentinels, caressed the fair princess, but struck the false courtier a blow that made him see the sun both in the east and west; then, seizing a piece of pastry, he ran off. Now there was a greater uproar than on the preceding day, and everyone wondered at what had taken place, excepting the king's daughter; for she again recognized her gold neck-chain, whereby she well knew who the dog's master was.

On the third day the youth wished to drink wine from the king's table and sent Snorium to fetch some. Everything now took place as before. The dog burst through the guard, entered the drinking apartment, caressed the princess, but struck the false courtier a blow that sent him tumbling head over heels on the floor; then, seizing a flask of wine, he ran off. The king was sorely vexed at all this, and sent the courtier with a number of people to seize the stranger who owned the three dogs. The courtier went, and came to where the young man dwelt with the poor fisherman. But there another game began; for the youth called to his three dogs: "Snipp! Snapp! Snorium! clear the house." In an instant the dogs rushed forward, and in a twinkling all the king's men lay on the ground.

The youth then caused the courtier to be bound hand and foot, and proceeded to the apartment where the king was sitting at table with his men. When he entered, the princess ran to meet him with great affection, and began relating to her father how the courtier had deceived him. When the king heard all this, and recognized his daughter's gold chain and ring, he ordered the courtier to be cast to the three dogs; but the brave youth obtained the princess, and with her half the kingdom.

BENJAMIN THORPE

The Enchanted Apple-tree

Flanders

Once upon a time there lived an old woman whose name was Misery.

Her one and only possession was an apple-tree and even this caused her more pain than pleasure. When the apples were ripe, the village urchins came and stole them off the tree.

This went on year after year, when one day an old man, with a long white beard, knocked at Misery's door. "Old woman," he begged, "give me a crust of bread."

"You, too, are a poor miserable creature," said Misery, who, although she had nothing herself, was full of compassion for others. "Here is half a loaf, take it; it is all I have, eat it in peace, and may it refresh you."

"As you have been so kind," said the old fellow, "I will grant you a wish."

"Oh!" sighed the old woman, "I have only one desire, that is, that anyone who touches my apple-tree may stick to it until I set them free. The way my apples are stolen from me is past all bearing."

"Your wish is granted," said the old fellow, and he went away.

Two days later Misery went to look at her tree; she found hanging and sticking to the branches a crowd of children, servants, mothers who had come to rescue their children, fathers who had tried to save their wives, two parrots who had escaped from their cage, a cock, a goose, an owl, and other birds, not to mention a goat. When she saw this extraordinary sight, she burst out laughing, and rubbed her hands with delight. She let them all remain hanging on the tree some time before she released them.

The thieves had learnt their lesson, and never stole the apples again.

Some time passed by, when one day someone again knocked at old Misery's door.

"Come in," she cried.

"Guess who I am," said a voice. "I am old Father Death himself. Listen, little mother," he continued. "I think that you and your old dog have lived long enough; I have come to fetch you both."

"You are all-powerful," said Misery. "I do not oppose your will, but before I pack up, grant me one favour. On the tree yonder there grow the most delicious apples you have ever tasted. Don't you think it would be a pity to leave them, without gathering one?"

"As you ask me so graciously, I will take one," said Death, whose mouth was watering as he walked towards the tree. He climbed up to the topmost branches to gather a large rosy apple, but directly he touched it, the wretch remained glued to the tree by his long bony hand. Nothing could tear him off, in spite of his struggles.

"There you are, old tyrant, hanging high and dry," said Misery.

As a result of Death hanging on the tree, no one died. If persons fell into the water they were not drowned; if a cart ran over them they did not even notice it; they did not die even if their heads were cut off.

After Death had hung, winter and summer, for ten long years on the tree, through all weathers, the old woman had pity on him, and allowed him to come down on condition that she should live as long as she liked.

This, Father Death agreed to, and that is why men live longer than the sparrows, and why Misery is always to be found in the world, and will doubtless remain until the end of time.

translated by M. C. O. MORRIS

True and Untrue

Norway

So long ago that we have lost count when, there was a poor widow, without a penny to scratch with, living in a bough-hung cottage at the edge of a great green forest in the Northlands. She had two sons, but though they were twins of a birth, no brothers were ever less alike than they. One was a kindly, generous, staunch-hearted lad whose name was True; the other was mean, cruel and sly, and looked for the truth only that he might sidle round it, so his name was Untrue. At length the day came when their mother said she could support them no longer, so with the clothes they stood up in and a packet of food to carry, off they went to seek their fortune.

"Don't worry, dear mother," said True at parting; "I am sure to get a good place and bring you back a hatful of gold."

But as for Untrue, he said nothing.

At least, he said nothing till they were making ready to eat their evening meal in the forest, when he sidled up to his brother, grinning like a stoat. "Brother," he said, "I am stronger than you, and would willingly carry the heavier load. So let us eat your food first, and when it is all gone, then we will eat mine, as is only fair."

So they ate True's food that evening and most of the following day, till it was all gone. Dusk found them still in the forest, and now it was time to start on Untrue's packet. But no, he said, he had only enough for one and never a crumb to spare. "And it is high time for us to part. I shall never get on in the world if I have to go shares with such a simpleton as you, brother True."

"Untrue by name, untrue by nature," said True. "You always have been and you always will be. Would you leave your own brother in the forest to starve?"

"With pleasure," Untrue assured him; and because he was the

stronger, and covetous to have all the world's fortune for himself, he rushed at his brother and before a jay could scream had plucked out both his eyes. "You see too much, with your true and untrue," he jeered. "Try seeing which is which now, you eyeless buzzard you!"

In blackness and pain True heard his brother's footsteps rustle into silence. "What shall I do?" he whispered. "I am blind and alone, and soon the dangers of the night will be upon me. Unless I can find some shelter or other I shall surely be dead by morning." Far off he heard a wolf howl and there was a crashing near at hand in the forest. He began to grope his way forward, with many a blow and stumble, till all at once he caught hold of the strong, odorous trunk of a big bushy lime tree. "I will climb into this tree, and its leaves will hide me," he told himself. "Then when the birds are singing again, or I feel the sun shine warm on my head, I shall know that it is morning and try to go a little farther." So he climbed up into the lime tree till he felt safe and then made himself as comfortable as he could among its friendly branches.

Not long afterwards he heard how someone came on delicate feet below him, and someone on strong, heavy feet, and then a third soft walker, and a fourth; and then he heard greetings and talk among them, and who should they be but Bruin the bear (it was not hard to tell when *he* sat down) and Long-ears the hare, together with Grey-legs the wolf and Sly-boots the fox (these last the two soft walkers), come up to keep St John's Eve under the tree. For a time they sat eating and drinking, and then they began to discuss some of their neighbours.

"These humans," said Bruin (it was not hard to tell when *he* was the speaker), "have less sense than you would think. Take their King now—he is so sand-blind that he cannot tell a hawk from a hedgehog, and yet if only he would come to this lime tree of ours in the morning and wet his eyes with the dew of its leaves he would have eyes so sharp that he could count the ladybird's spots at the end of his garden."

"Their ignorance is not even their bliss," agreed Sly-boots. "I never slink past his palace unless he is grumbling and grousing about the drinking-water there; and indeed it is so muddy and full of curlywigs that I would rather go thirsty than touch it. Yet if only he would dig up the big stone in his palace yard he would find a spring of the coolest, cleanest, brightest water in the world."

"There's his orchard too," piped up Long-ears. "It should be the noblest in the whole country, but if he gets a green crab or withered pear, that is the sum of it. Yet if only he would dig up the triple gold chain that lies in the ground all round it he would have apples and pears to make your mouth water."

"Poor old fellow that he is," added Grey-legs. "I don't know whether to pity him or his daughter most. She is a pretty girl enough, and amiable too, but deaf as a post and dumb as a shovel. How will he ever marry her off, I wonder? Yet if he only knew it she could be cured in a whiffy. Last year when she went to Communion she let a crumb of the bread fall from her mouth to the ground, and up came a big warty toad and swallowed it. Now if they would only dig up the chancel floor they would find that toad squatting under the altar rails. All they would then need to do is tickle him under the throat till he spits up the crumb, and the minute the Princess swallows that crumb she will talk and hear with the best of them."

"Well, it only goes to show," concluded Bruin wisely, and since they had now emptied their bottles and finished their honey, sorrel and marrow, True heard them bid each other a satisfied good night and take themselves off, thump-thump, slip-slide, or pit-a-pat, pat.

As can be imagined, True was far too excited to sleep, and if a lime tree had thorns he would certainly have been on them till morning. But when the first birds tossed their little songs in air he reached out his hand to the leaves and wetted his eyes with the dew he found on them, and it was just as Bruin said: he could see as he had never seen before. He could count the veins in the farthest lime leaves or number the toenails of a high-flying eagle. "If this is true, then all is true," he told himself, and before a mouse could run up a wheat-stalk he set off for the King's palace.

That very morning it happened that the King had gone walking in his yard, and towards noon, as the sun rode high, he grew so dry and thirsty that he called for a glass of water. A courtier brought him one, all fal-de-lals and furbelows, but, "Fooh!" groaned the King when he held it near to his eyes and saw the mud and wrigglies in it, "what sort of king am I, that with all my crowns and sceptres, and men to run here and men to run there, I cannot get a glass of clean water when I am thirsty?"

"Why, Your Majesty," said True, stepping briskly forward, "if you would just lend me some of those same men to dig up the big stone I see here, you would have water bright as crystal and fresher than a harebell."

So it proved, for as they lifted up the stone there spurted forth a spring of water so clear that where its jet broke and spread in air it was like looking at a spray of diamonds from a queen's hand. And when the King had taken only one glassful, so bright and pure and cellar-cool was the draught that he made True clerk of the royal waterworks, with power over sluices and conduits, culverts and pumps.

A few days later the King was in the palace yard drinking glass after glass of that lovely water when a hawk came swooping down upon his chickens. "There he goes!" cried the courtiers. "Oh, what a ruffian!" The King called for his musket and it was placed in the royal hand, but by this time the hawk was flying off with the fattest pullet of them all, and the King's eyesight was so bad that all he destroyed when he blazed away was three wigs and a window. "If only there was someone who could cure my eyes," moaned the King, "for I fear I shall soon grow quite blind!"

"Leave it to me, Your Majesty, sir," said True, stepping quickly forward; and he told him the story of how he had recovered his own sight. Within the hour the King set off for the lime tree, and in the morning as the first birds tossed their little songs in air he wetted his eyes with dew from the leaves and was soon counting the legs of a distant caterpillar. Then and there he appointed True master of the royal spectacles, with power over visions and shows, sights (including insights) and illusions.

Some weeks later the King and True were walking in the royal orchard when the King said: "Tell me, True, what sort of king am I, that with all my horses and men I cannot grow more than a green crab or withered pear throughout the length and breadth of this great orchard?"

"Your Majesty, sir," said True, stepping respectfully alongside, "if you will give me what lies thrice round your orchard, and lend me men to dig it up, your orchard will grow apples sweeter than wine and pears the size of pumpkins."

So it proved, for once they had dug up the triple gold chain, goodness flowed back into the soil, and soon the boughs of the trees hung down to the ground with apples and pears of such size and succulence that no one had ever tasted the like. One whole round of the gold chain True gave to the King, and almost as much he sent home to his mother. With what was left he became the richest commoner in the kingdom, and the King, who had a strong sense of fitness, made him keeper of the royal links.

Not long afterwards the King and True were eating apples and settling State affairs when the poor deaf-and-dumb Princess walked past them in her downcast way. "Friend True," said the King, "I would give half my kingdom and my daughter as well to the man who could cure her of her affliction. And if you were that man," he went on hopefully, "my happiness would be complete."

"Leave it to me, Your Majesty, sir," replied True, and when he had borrowed a dozen of the King's men, together with their picks, crowbars, mandrils and shovels, he went into the church and dug up the chancel floor. There under the altar rails they found the big toad, warts and all, and when they had tickled his throat with a feather up came the crumb, just as Grey-legs had said, and the self-same moment the King's daughter swallowed that crumb she could talk and hear with any princess alive.

So now there was to be a wedding of True and the Princess, with cakes and wine and dancing and all such mirth as the heart can long for or the head devise. The revelry was at its gayest, and the dancers whirling their fastest, when a beggar lad looked in at the doorway, so ragged, spiteful and cruel-eyed that all who saw him drew back and crossed themselves. True looked at him and for all his tatters knew him at once. It was Untrue his brother.

"Do you not know me again?" he asked, stepping sternly before him.

"How should a poor beggar like me know a rich lord like you?" whined Untrue.

"Untrue by name, untrue by nature," said True. "I am True your brother, whose eyes you plucked out a year ago to-day." But when Untrue started back in terror, he added gently enough: "Still, you *are* my brother, and you shall have food of the best and new clothes, and after that you can go to the lime tree where I sat this night last year. If you hear anything to your advantage there, it is a sign that you have repented, and that Providence is willing to help you. So good luck go with you!"

Then and there Untrue set off for the lime tree. Full of cake and wine and with new clothes on his back, he was soon as brazen as ever. "Why," he told himself, rubbing his hands in glee, "if that simpleton brother of mine could learn enough in a night-time there to become king of half the country, what should I not learn—sharp and crafty as I am?" He climbed up into the tree and sat on one of its biggest branches, and in an hour or so he heard how someone came along on delicate feet, and someone on strong heavy ones, and then a third and a fourth soft walker, till there they were, Bruin and Long-ears, Grey-legs and Sly-boots, come with their bags and their bottles to keep St John's Eve under the tree. Soon they had finished eating, and Untrue's ears spread wide as a bat's wings as he hoped to learn some helpful secrets; but all he could hear was Bruin saying that he was still quite hungry, and Grey-legs agreeing that he felt sharpish too. Sly-boots and Long-ears then began murmuring something, and Untrue kept leaning farther and farther off his bough in order to catch their words. That was why he fell out of the tree, and that in its turn was why Bruin and Grey-legs were not in the least hungry or sharpish when at last they said good night and the animals went their separate ways. And finally, that was why no one in the kingdom was ever again plagued by Untrue, and why True and his Princess knew never a care and lived happy as birds ever after.

retold by GWYN JONES

The Elf Maiden

Lapland

Once upon a time two young men living in a small village fell in love with the same girl. During the winter, it was all night except for an hour or so about noon, when the darkness seemed a little less dark, and then they used to see which of them could tempt her out for a sleigh ride with the Northern Lights flashing above them, or which could persuade her to come to a dance in some neighbouring barn. But when the spring began, and the light grew longer, the hearts of the villagers leapt at the sight of the sun, and a day was fixed for the boats to be brought out, and the great nets to be spread in the bays of some islands that lay a few miles to the north. Everybody went on this expedition, and the two young men and the girl went with them.

They all sailed merrily across the sea chattering like a flock of magpies, or singing their favourite songs. And when they reached the shore, what an unpacking there was! For this was a noted fishing ground, and here they would live, in little wooden huts, till autumn and bad weather came round again.

The maiden and the two young men happened to share the same hut with some friends, and fished daily from the same boat. And as time went on, one of the youths remarked that the girl took less notice of him than she did of his companion. At first he tried to think that he was dreaming, and for a long while he kept his eyes shut very tight to what he did not want to see, but in spite of his efforts, the truth managed to wriggle through, and then the young man gave up trying to deceive himself, and set about finding some way to get the better of his rival.

The plan that he hit upon could not be carried out for some months; but the longer the young man thought of it, the more pleased he was with it, so he made no sign of his feelings, and waited patiently till the moment came. This was the very day that they were all going to leave the islands, and sail back to the mainland for the winter. In the bustle and hurry of departure, the cunning fisherman contrived that their boat should be the last to put off, and when everything was ready, and the sails about to be set, he suddenly called out:

"Oh, dear, what shall I do! I have left my best knife behind in the hut. Run, like a good fellow, and get it for me, while I raise the anchor and loosen the tiller."

Not thinking any harm, the youth jumped back on shore and made his way up the steep bank. At the door of the hut he stopped and looked back, then started and gazed in horror. The head of the boat stood out to sea, and he was left alone on the island.

Yes, there was no doubt of it—he was quite alone; and he had nothing to help him except the knife which his comrade had purposely dropped on the ledge of the window. For some minutes he was too stunned by the treachery of his friend to think about anything at all, but after a while he shook himself awake, and determined that he would manage to keep alive somehow, if it were only to revenge himself.

So he put the knife in his pocket and went off to a part of the island which was not so bare as the rest, and had a small grove of trees. From one of these he cut himself a bow, which he strung with a piece of cord that had been left lying about the huts.

When this was ready the young man ran down to the shore and shot one or two sea-birds, which he plucked and cooked for supper.

In this way the months slipped by, and Christmas came round again. The evening before, the youth went down to the rocks and into the copse, collecting all the driftwood the sea had washed up or the gale had blown down, and he piled it up in a great stack outside the door, so that he might not have to fetch any all the next day. As soon as his task was done, he paused and looked out towards the mainland, thinking of Christmas Eve last year, and the merry dance they had had. The night was still and cold, and by the help of the Northern Lights he could almost see across to the opposite coast, when, suddenly, he noticed a boat, which seemed steering straight for the island. At first he could hardly stand for joy, the chance of speaking to another man was so delightful; but as the boat drew near there was something, he could not tell what, that was different from the boats which he had been used to all his life, and when it touched the shore he saw that the people that filled it were beings of another world than ours. Then he hastily stepped behind the wood stack, and waited for what might happen next.

The strange folk one by one jumped on to the rocks, each bearing a load of something that they wanted. Among the women he remarked two young girls, more beautiful and better dressed than any of the rest, carrying between them two great baskets full of provisions. The young man peeped out cautiously to see what all this crowd could be doing inside the tiny hut, but in a moment he drew back again, as the girls returned, and looked about as if they wanted to find out what sort of a place the island was.

Their sharp eyes soon discovered the form of a man crouching behind the bundles of sticks, and at first they felt a little frightened, and started as if they would run away. But the youth remained so still, that they took courage and laughed gaily to each other. "What a strange creature, let us try what he is made of," said one, and she stooped down and gave him a pinch.

Now the young man had a pin sticking in the sleeve of his jacket, and the moment the girl's hand touched him she pricked it so sharply that the blood came. The girl screamed so loudly that the people all ran out of their huts to see what was the matter. But directly they caught sight of the man they turned and fled in the other direction, and picking up the goods they had brought with them scampered as fast as they could down to the shore. In an instant, boat, people, and goods had vanished completely.

In their hurry they had, however, forgotten two things: a bundle of keys which lay on the table, and the girl whom the pin had pricked, and who now stood pale and helpless beside the wood stack.

"You will have to make me your wife," she said at last, "for you have drawn my blood, and I belong to you."

"Why not? I am quite willing," answered he. "But how do you suppose we can manage to live till summer comes round again?"

"Do not be anxious about that," said the girl; "if you will only marry me all will be well. I am very rich, and all my family are rich also."

Then the young man gave her his promise to make her his wife, and the girl fulfilled her part of the bargain, and food was plentiful on the island all through the long winter months, though he never knew how it got there. And by-and-by it was spring once more, and time for the fisher-folk to sail from the mainland.

"Where are we to go now?" asked the girl, one day, when the sun seemed brighter and the wind softer than usual.

"I do not care where I go," answered the young man; "what do you think?"

The girl replied that she would like to go somewhere right at the other end of the island, and build a house, far away from the huts of the fishing folk. And he consented, and that very day they set off in search of a sheltered spot on the banks of a stream, so that it would be easy to get water.

In a tiny bay, on the opposite side of the island, they found the very thing, which seemed to have been made on purpose for them; and as they were tired with their long walk, they laid themselves down on a bank of moss among some birches and prepared to have a good night's rest, so as to be fresh for work next day. But before she went to sleep the girl turned to her husband, and said: "If in your dreams you fancy that you hear strange noises, be sure you do not stir, or get up to see what it is."

"Oh, it is not likely we shall hear any noises in such a quiet place," answered he, and fell sound asleep.

Suddenly he was awakened by a great clatter about his ears, as if all the workmen in the world were sawing and hammering and building close to him. He was just going to spring up and go to see what it meant, when he luckily remembered his wife's words and lay still. But the time till morning seemed very long, and with the first ray of sun they both rose, and pushed aside the branches of the birch trees. There, in the very place they had chosen, stood a beautiful house—doors and windows, and everything all complete!

"Now you must fix on a spot for your cow-stalls," said the girl, when they had breakfasted off wild cherries; "and take care it is the proper size, neither too large nor too small." And the husband did as he was bid, though he wondered what use a cow-house could be, as they had no cows to put in it. But as he was a little afraid of his wife, who knew so much more than he, he asked no questions.

This night also he was awakened by the same sounds as before, and in the morning they found, near the stream, the most beautiful cow-house that ever was seen, with stalls and milk-pails and stools all complete, indeed, everything that a cow-house could possibly want, except the cows. Then the girl bade him measure out the ground for a storehouse, and this, she said, might be as large as he pleased; and when the storehouse was ready she proposed that they should set off to pay her parents a visit.

The old people welcomed them heartily, and summoned their neighbours, for many miles round, to a great feast in their honour. In fact, for several weeks there was no work done on the farm at all; and at length the young man and his wife grew tired of so much play and declared that they must return to their own home. But, before they started on the journey, the wife whispered to her husband: "Take care to jump over the threshold as quick as you can, or it will be the worse for you."

The young man listened to her words, and sprang over the threshold like an arrow from a bow; and it was well he did, for, no sooner was he on the other side, than his father-in-law threw a great hammer at him, which would have broken both his legs, if it had only touched them.

When they had gone some distance on the road home, the girl turned to her husband and said: "Till you step inside the house, be sure you do not look back, whatever you may hear or see."

And the husband promised, and for a while all was still; and he thought no more about the matter till he noticed at last that the nearer he drew to the house the louder grew the noise of the trampling of feet behind him. As he laid his hand upon the door he thought he was safe, and turned to look. There, sure enough, was a vast herd of cattle, which had been sent after him by his father-in-law when he found that his daughter had been cleverer than he. Half of the herd were already through the fence and cropping the grass on the banks of the stream, but half still remained outside and faded into nothing, even as he watched them.

However, enough cattle were left to make the young man rich, and he and his wife lived happily together, except that every now and then the girl vanished from his sight, and never told him where she had been. For a long time he kept silence about it; but one day, when he had been complaining of her absence, she said to him: "Dear husband, I am bound to go, even against my will, and there is only one way to stop me. Drive a nail into the threshold, and then I can never pass in or out."

And so he did.

retold by ANDREW LANG

The King o' the Cats

England

One winter's evening the sexton's wife was sitting by the fireside with her big black cat, Old Tom, on the other side, both half asleep and waiting for the master to come home. They waited and they waited, but still he didn't come, till at last he came rushing in, calling out, "Who's Tommy Tildrum?" in such a wild way that both his wife and his cat stared at him to know what was the matter.

"Why, what's the matter?" said his wife, "and why do you want to know who Tommy Tildrum is?"

"Oh, I've had such an adventure. I was digging away at old Mr Fordyce's grave when I suppose I must have dropped asleep, and only woke up by hearing a cat's *Miaou*."

"*Miaou!*" said Old Tom in answer.

"Yes, just like that! So I looked over the edge of the grave, and what do you think I saw?"

"Now, how can I tell?" said the sexton's wife.

"Why, nine black cats all like our friend Tom here, all with a white spot on their chestesses. And what do you think they were carrying? Why, a small coffin covered with a black velvet pall, and on the pall was a small coronet all of gold, and at every third step they took they cried all together, *Miaou*—"

"*Miaou!*" said Old Tom again.

"Yes, just like that!" said the sexton; "and as they came nearer and nearer to me I could see them more distinctly, because their eyes shone out with a sort of green light. Well, they all came towards me, eight of them carrying the coffin, and the biggest cat of all walking in front for all the world like—but look at our Tom, how he's looking at me. You'd think he knew all I was saying."

"Go on, go on," said his wife; "never mind Old Tom."

"Well, as I was a-saying, they came towards me slowly and solemnly, and at every third step crying all together, *Miaou*—"

"*Miaou!*" said Old Tom again.

"Yes, just like that, till they came and stood right opposite Mr Fordyce's grave, where I was, when they all stood still and looked straight at me. I did feel queer, that I did! But look at Old Tom; he's looking at me just like they did."

"Go on, go on," said his wife; "never mind Old Tom."

"Where was I? Oh, they all stood still looking at me, when the one that wasn't carrying the coffin came forward and, staring straight at me, said to me—yes, I tell 'ee, *said* to me, with a squeaky voice, "Tell Tom Tildrum that Tim Toldrum's dead," and that's why I asked you if you knew who Tom Tildrum was, for how can I tell Tom Tildrum Tim Toldrum's dead if I don't know who Tom Tildrum is?"

"Look at Old Tom, look at Old Tom!" screamed his wife.

And well he might look, for Tom was swelling and Tom was staring, and at last Tom shrieked out, "What—old Tim dead! then I'm the King o' the Cats!" and rushed up the chimney and was never more seen.

retold by JOSEPH JACOBS

Little Annie the Goose-girl

Norway

Once upon a time there was a King who had so many geese, he was forced to have a lassie to tend them and watch them; her name was Annie, and so they called her "Annie the goose-girl". Now you must know there was a King's son from England who went out to woo; and as he came along Annie sat herself down in his way.

"Sitting all alone there, you little Annie?" said the King's son.

"Yes," said little Annie, "here I sit and put stitch to stitch, and patch on patch. I'm waiting to-day for the King's son from England."

"Him you mustn't look to have," said the Prince.

"Nay, but if I'm to have him," said little Annie, "have him I shall after all."

And now limners were sent out into all lands and realms to take the likenesses of the fairest Princesses, and the Prince was to choose between them. So he thought so much of one of them, that he set out to seek her, and wanted to wed her, and he was glad and happy when he got her for his sweetheart.

But now I must tell you this Prince had a stone with him which he laid by his bedside, and that stone knew everything, and when the Princess came little Annie told her, if so be she'd had a sweetheart before, or didn't feel herself quite free from anything which she didn't wish the Prince to know, she'd better not step on that stone which lay by the bedside.

"If you do, it will tell him all about you," said little Annie.

So when the Princess heard that she was dreadfully downcast, and she fell upon the thought to ask Annie if she would get into bed that night in her stead and lie down by the Prince's side, and then when he was sound asleep, Annie should get out and the Princess should get in, and so when he woke up in the morning he would find the right bride by his side.

So they did that, and when Annie the goose-girl came and stepped upon the stone the Prince asked—

"Who is this that steps into my bed?"

"A maid pure and bright," said the stone, and so they lay down to sleep; but when the night wore on the Princess came and lay down in Annie's stead.

But next morning, when they were to get up, the Prince asked the stone again—

"Who is this that steps out of my bed?"

"One that has had three bairns," said the stone.

When the Prince heard that he wouldn't have her, you may know very well; and so he packed her off home again, and took another sweetheart.

But as he went to see her, Annie went and sat down in his way again.

"Sitting all alone there, little Annie the goose-girl," said the Prince.

"Yes, here I sit, and put stitch to stitch, and patch to patch; for I'm waiting to-day for the King's son from England," said Annie.

"Oh! you mustn't look to have him," said the King's son.

"Nay, but if I'm to have him, have him I shall, after all"; that was what Annie thought.

Well, it was the same story over again with the Prince; only this time, when his bride got up in the morning, the stone said she'd had six bairns.

So the Prince wouldn't have her either, but sent her about her business; but still he thought he'd try once more if he couldn't find one who was pure and spotless; and he sought far and wide in many lands, till at last he found one he thought he might trust. But when he went to see her, little Annie the goose-girl had put herself in his way again.

"Sitting all alone there, you little Annie the goose-girl," said the Prince.

"Yes, here I sit, and put stitch to stitch, and patch to patch; for I'm waiting to-day for the King's son from England," said Annie.

"Him you mustn't look to have," said the Prince.

"Nay, but if I'm to have him, have him I shall, after all," said little Annie.

So when the Princess came, little Annie the goose-girl told her the same as she had told the other two, if she'd had any sweetheart before, or if there was anything else she didn't wish the Prince to know, she mustn't tread on the stone that the Prince had put at his bedside; for, said she—

"It tells him everything."

The Princess got very red and downcast when she heard that, for she was just as naughty as the others, and asked Annie if she would go in her stead and lie down with the Prince that night; and when he was sound asleep, she would come and take her place, and then he would have the right bride by his side when it was light next morning.

Yes! they did that. And when little Annie the goose-girl came and stepped upon the stone, the Prince asked—

"Who is this that steps into my bed?"

"A maid pure and bright," said the stone; and so they lay down to rest.

Farther on in the night the Prince put a ring on Annie's finger, and it fitted so tight she couldn't get it off again; for the Prince saw well enough there was something wrong, and so he wished to have a mark by which he might know the right woman again.

Well, when the Prince had gone off to sleep, the Princess came and drove Annie away to the pigsty, and lay down in her place. Next morning, when they were to get up, the Prince asked—

"Who is this that steps out of my bed?"

"One that's had nine bairns," said the stone.

When the Prince heard that he drove her away at once, for he was in an awful rage; and then he asked the stone how it all was with these Princesses who had stepped on it, for he couldn't understand it at all, he said.

So the stone told him how they had cheated him, and sent little Annie the goose-girl to him in their stead.

But as the Prince wished to have no mistake about it, he went down to her where she sat tending her geese, for he wanted to see if she had the ring too, and he thought, "if she has it, 'twere best to take her at once for my queen".

So when he got down he saw in a moment that she had tied a bit of rag round one of her fingers, and so he asked her why it was tied up.

"Oh! I've cut myself so badly," said little Annie the goose-girl.

So he must and would see the finger, but Annie wouldn't take the rag off. Then he caught hold of the finger; but Annie, she tried to pull it from him, and so between them the rag came off, and then he knew his ring.

So he took her up to the palace, and gave her much fine clothes and attire, and after that they held their wedding feast; and so little Annie the goose-girl came to have the King of England's son for her husband after all, just because it was written that she should have him.

collected by PETER CHRISTEN ASBJÖRNSEN and JÖRGEN I. MOE
translated by Sir George Webbe Dasent

The Troll Ride

Sweden

Peder Lars, the young son of a farmer, came riding along the highway.

His heart was gay. He was bound for the city to buy a new jacket because that evening he was going a-courting and wanted to look his best. And he felt rather sure that he would not be turned down. However proud and rich Lisa was, and even though Peder Lars was the poorest of all her admirers, she had looked at him kindly. His spokesman had extracted a promise that he and his father might come to her at six that afternoon to state their intentions.

Peder Lars rode across fields through a long deep forest, then he emerged from the forest on to a green meadow. Suddenly he saw something that seemed to be moving in a ditch. He drew nearer, and realized it was a strange-looking woman, crawling along.

She lifted her head and stared at him. He had never before seen anything as ugly and evil-looking as her face. Her small peppercorn eyes were almost hidden in matted hair. Her nose looked like a carrot, and her lips were brown as bread crust.

"Will you do me a good turn?" she asked. "I shall reward you for your trouble."

"What is it?" asked Peder Lars.

The woman said that she had hurt her leg wandering in the forest, and had limped this far because, in the next wood, near a path that climbed a hill, there grew seven pine trees. A little resin from each of these pines rubbed into her wound would make the pain go away immediately. But before she got very far from the forest she had collapsed, and so was lying here helpless in the ditch. She badly needed someone to collect resin from the wood for her. She would see that he was well rewarded for his trouble. Already, five people had accepted a gold coin for saying they would help, but they had probably enjoyed themselves with the money and taken another road home, because she had not seen any of them again, although she had been lying in the ditch since early morning. She held up a brightly shining gold coin before Peder Lars and said she would give it to him if he would fetch the resin.

Peder Lars stepped back. "Who are you that look so evil and have so many gold coins?"

She moaned, and rubbed her leg. "Oh, how it hurts! And my mother is walking in the forest looking for me, and calling me. Listen, can you hear?"

"No, I don't hear anything," said Peder Lars. But then the woman grabbed the mane of his horse, pulled herself up, and put her hand like a trumpet to his ear. Now he heard someone singing deep in the forest.

Where are you, daughter, sweet and fair?
I'm looking for you everywhere.

Peder Lars could not help laughing, because he did not think that "sweet and fair" really suited the ugly one by his side. "Sweet and fair," he repeated, chuckling.

The woman sank rapidly back into the ditch again. But she kept her head over the edge, and her small peppercorn eyes shot fiery glances.

"You laugh like all the rest," she hissed, "and hate me! But I will give you money, as much money as you want, if only you will get me that pine resin." And she rattled the gold coins in her fist.

Peder Lars stared at her. Then he knocked her hand so that all the gold coins fell into the ditch.

"No, thank you," he said. "You are a troll, and I don't want to have anything to do with a troll." And he cracked his whip and continued his journey.

He rode into the city, bought himself a gay jacket, and turned homewards again. When he came to the hill that the woman had mentioned, he could not help looking around for the seven pine trees. There they stood in a row, murmuring softly. At that moment he heard someone singing far, far away:

Where are you, daughter, sweet and fair?
I'm looking for you everywhere.

He looked up the pine trunks to see if there really was any resin to be found. But it would have been impossible to find it without looking carefully, now that the afternoon light was fading.

No, I must hurry, he thought, or I'll reach Lisa late, and that might cost me dearly, proud and particular as she is. And so he rode on.

He had gone only a little farther when his horse stopped by itself and pricked up its ears, listening. Once again he heard the song:

> *Where are you, daughter, sweet and fair?*
> *I'm looking for you everywhere.*

If only I had time to gather some of that resin, he thought, and turned around. But after a minute he changed his mind. "It's madness," he said to himself. "What do I care about an ugly old troll woman?" And so he turned homewards again.

It did not take long before the horse stopped again and once more he heard the song:

> *Where are you, daughter, sweet and fair?*
> *I'm looking for you everywhere.*

I can't bear it, thought Peder Lars. If I don't get the resin, I'm afraid I will never stop hearing that song. And so he galloped back to the pine trees.

He examined the trunks and branches, and did at last succeed in gathering resin from each of the seven trees. By now it was almost dark, and he began to gallop along the road. He came to the ditch and saw the troll woman still sitting there.

"Here you are, you ugly old hag," he shouted, throwing the resin into her lap. "And I hope I never see you again, for you have probably cost me my sweetheart's hand."

He spurred his horse on without waiting to hear whether she would thank him or not. He was angry and anxious, sure that he would be too late. And then what would Lisa's father say? Peder Lars knew he wasn't too happy to have a pauper for a son-in-law. And Lisa herself? Her pride might be hurt.

Suddenly he heard the tramp of horses' hooves nearby, and from round a bend in the road a rider approached him. It was his brother. He looked a sight, and his horse was all in a lather.

"You'll be late, you'll be late!" his brother called. And as the two of them galloped on together, he told Peder Lars that he and their old

father and the spokesman had been waiting by Lisa's farm-gate for
Peder Lars to come, when suddenly the rich miller Jonas, who
owned half the village, had pulled up in his carriage. He, too, was
going in to ask for the beautiful Lisa's hand. When miller Jonas
heard that Peder Lars was expected at six o'clock, he was not at all
dismayed. If Peder Lars was turned down, he said, then he was ready
to take his place. And so there he sat now, waiting. By the time Peder
Lars and his brother met on the road it was a quarter to six and they
had several miles to go.

"Good-bye," Peder Lars called, urging his horse to the utmost and
streaking along the forest path at break-neck speed. It was so dark
that he could hardly see the road before him. Branches tore at his
handsome new jacket, and scratched his forehead until it bled, but he
paid no attention. All Peder Lars could think of was that the beautiful Lisa might give her hand to the rich miller Jonas so as to punish
him for being late. That was what you got for having anything to do
with trolls.

Soon his horse began to pant and stumble and trip, and Peder Lars
was afraid it might collapse under him. The horse went slower and
slower, no matter how he urged it forward.

Then he felt the reins stiffen and go taut in his hands. The horse
lifted its head, and its hooves began to fly over the ground. Something seemed to have brought it back to life, and it went so fast that
Peder Lars's cape was billowing behind.

Peder Lars turned round in the saddle. It seemed to him that
someone was sitting behind him on the horse's back. No one was
there, though, and yet he imagined he saw what looked like a grey
bundle slip down over the horse's rump.

The ride became wilder and wilder. Peder Lars no longer felt in
control of the reins, now the horse no longer followed the road, but
turned in among bushes and undergrowth. It jumped hillocks and
streams, and every time Peder Lars cast a look behind, he dimly
glimpsed a grey bundle sliding farther back on the horse. And every
time he looked ahead, he felt more and more sure that someone was
sitting behind him.

They had reached open fields now, and the cape was flying straight
up over his head, stretched as trim as a sail. The horse flew like a bird
and its hooves barely touched ground. At the first fork in the road,
Peder Lars met his spokesman, who had run out to find him and urge
him to hurry.

"You are too late, Peder Lars!" shouted the spokesman. "Only
five minutes are left."

"We'll see," Peder Lars called, and was gone in a wink.

A little farther on he met his old father, who shook his head sadly. "You will never get there. You have only a minute left."

"We'll see," Peder Lars called, and disappeared so fast that the old man did not even see him go.

At the farmer's house everyone was waiting. Beautiful Lisa, her arm leaning on the window-sill, was listening for the beat of hooves, while her father and the miller rubbed their hands contentedly.

"Now," said her father looking at the clock on the wall. "There is only half a minute to go. And if he were going to come on time, we would have heard his horse on the bridge by now. Lisa, you may as well give the miller your hand right away, for you would never be satisfied with a suitor who kept you waiting."

"I will wait until six o'clock," Lisa said. She stood there with beating heart. For though she was so proud that she would rather have made herself unhappy for the rest of her life than be kept waiting a single second by a suitor, it would be desperately hard to lose Peder Lars.

The clock began to chime.

"Too late!" cried the miller.

The strong beat of hooves was heard on the bridge just then, and Lisa's eyes shone with joy.

"Listen, he is coming!" she exclaimed.

"Too late, though," said her father.

But just as the clock was ready to chime for the sixth time, the door was flung open and there stood Peder Lars, dripping wet, his hair tousled, and his new jacket dusty and torn. Somehow he looked jaunty and dashing all the same. Lisa ran to him and put her hand in his, so firmly and confidently that he knew she was giving it to him for life.

The miller and the farmer could only gape. They could not understand how Peder Lars had managed to arrive on time, and no one else understood either.

But this was not the last time people would marvel at Peder Lars. From then on, regardless of how late he set out on any journey, he would always arrive on time, and no one ever saw him anxious to get started. Whether he rode on horseback or in a carriage, he was calm and assured. And he could well afford to be, for he always felt he had someone with him, someone who held the bridle and reins in such a way that all his adventures always finished well. But who this was he never could discover, no matter how many times he thought he glimpsed a grey bundle slip down the rump of his horse or off the

edge of his carriage the moment he turned his head. Yet inside
himself Peder Lars knew who it was that sat behind him.

He had not asked any reward for what he had done for the troll in
the ditch, but for all that, it had been an honest troll, and a reward he
certainly did receive.

retold by ANNA WAHLENBERG
translated by Holger Lundbergh

꜅꜅꜅꜅꜅꜅꜅꜅꜅꜅꜅꜅꜅꜅꜅꜅꜅꜅ ꜅꜅꜅꜅꜅꜅꜅꜅꜅꜅꜅꜅꜅꜅꜅꜅꜅꜅꜅꜅꜅꜅꜅

Annie Norn and the Fin Folk
Orkney

꜅꜅

Pretty Annie Norn lived many years ago on the mainland of Orkney. One evening, she went to the shore at twilight for salt water to boil the supper in. (At that time, salt was scarce and very dear.) But she never returned. Friends and family sought her far and near, searched up and down, along the shores and the sands, by the crags and the geo,* through field and furrow. But never a trace of Annie Norn did they find.

"The Trows have taken her," whispered some.

"The Fin Folk have carried her off," said others. And all the older people of the island warned their children once again never to venture out on the shore between the lines of high and low water when the sun was down. For the Fairy Folk and the Fin Folk and all kinds of spirits have power when daylight is passing into darkness; and the edges of land and forest and sea are unchancy places at any time.

Three or four years later, an Orkney vessel was coming home from Norway in the fall of the year. One of the sailors, Willie Norn, was a cousin of Annie's. Midway in its voyage, the vessel was caught in a violent tempest, and tossed to and fro for weeks in the North Sea until the crew were thoroughly exhausted. Their food and water was nearly all gone, and they had lost all sense of their bearing, for neither sun nor star was to be seen. Even when the storm abated after many days, a thick mist lay on the sea, and the men could not tell where they were nor what direction they should steer.

Then a small cool wind arose, but instead of making headway when the sails were trimmed, the ship stood still. The men lamented

* A creek.

loudly, saying that they were bewitched, and that their end would be to die there in a rotting hulk on this enchanted sea. In the midst of their outcry, a small boat drew alongside, rowed by one woman.

"A Fin Wife! A Fin Wife!" they cried in terror.

"Ask her to sell us a wind," suggested one bolder than the rest.

"If she comes aboard we are doomed and sunk!" muttered another.

While they argued, the woman sprang over the tafferel like a cat, and stood on deck. And Willie Norn started and stared, and cried,

"Annie, lass! Is this truly thee, Annie?"

"Oh ay!" says she. "How's all the folk at home, Willie? Ay, lad, if blood were not thicker than water you had not seen me here this day."

Then she turned to the crew.

"You great fools!" she cried. "Why do you stand there gaping an' glowering at me as if I were a witch?"

And she bade them bring the vessel about, and took the helm herself, and called her orders as if she had been a born skipper. And when the ship got on the other tack, she made fine headway. In a little, the fog brightened ahead. Then it lifted, and the ship was lying in a land-locked bay calm as a lake. Beautiful hills and green valleys ran back from the shores all around. Many streams gushed sparkling down the hillsides, murmuring as they wimpled to the sea. Our Lady's hens, the skylarks, sang so loud that it seemed the very sky showered music down. This was part of Hilda-Land, the home of the Fin Folk above the waves, that is usually invisible to men. To the weary, storm-tossed sailors, it seemed a perfect heaven.

Annie took the men on shore and led them up to a grand house, saying it was her home.

"By my faith, lass," says Willie, her cousin, "it's no wonder that you left Orkney, for you're well off here!"

"Oh, Willie," says Annie, "it's refreshing to hear an oath once more, for I never heard an oath or any swearing since I left my own human kind. No, no! Fin Folk don't spend their breath in swearing. And, boys, I tell you all, you had best not swear while in Hilda-Land! And mind well—while you are here, a close tongue keeps a safe head."

Then she took the men into the big hall and gave them plenty of meat and drink. And then she showed them to beds, and they slept they did not know how long. When they awoke there was a great feast prepared for them. All the neighbouring Fin Men were bidden, and came riding on sea-horses.

Annie's goodman sat in the high seat and bade the mariners hearty welcome to Hilda-Land. When the feast was ended, Annie said to them that they should go on board the ship and make for home.

But the skipper said that he did not know which way to steer.

"Take no thought for that," said his host. "We will give you a pilot. His boat lies alongside your ship now. Each of you must throw a silver shilling into the boat as pilot's fee."

Then they went down to the shore. Annie and Willie Norn walked behind, talking about old times. And many a kind message Annie sent to her own folk. Willie pressed her to come home with him, but she refused.

"No, no," she said. "I'm over well-off here to think of leaving. And tell my mother I have three bonnie bairns."

Then she drew from her pocket a token tied to a string of otter's hair, and gave it to Willie.

"I know you were courting Mary Foubister, and she's not sure of taking you, for she has many offers. But when you get home, hang this token about her neck, and I warrant she'll like you better than any other."

The men said farewell to Annie on the beach, and her husband rowed them to the ship. Each of the crew flung his silver shilling into the pilot's boat alongside. One dark-faced Fin Man sat in it, and as the silver fell, he laughed, for the Fin Men dearly love silver money. When they had all got on board and were to say farewell to Annie's husband, he says—

"O my good friends, I have long wished to see men playing at cards. Will ye play one game with me before sailing?"

"That we will, and welcome!" says the skipper. "I have a pack in the locker below."

So they all went below, dealt out, and began playing cards in the cabin. Now it may be that the parting-cup at the end of the Fin Men's feast was drugged, or it may be that the Fin Folk had wrought some of their spells, I do not know. But before the third trick was turned, every one of the Orkney crew sank into a heavy sleep, some lying with their heads on the table and some sprawled on the lockers. And there they slept and slept, none knew how long—it might have been hours or it might have been days.

The skipper was the first to wake. Rubbing his eyes, he ran up the ladder, and as he stuck his head out of the companionway, the first thing he clapped eyes on was the Crag of Gaitnup. He roused his men, and as they came on deck, they saw with joy that the vessel was anchored safe and snug in Scapa Bay, and the morning sun was glinting on the weather-cock of the spire of Saint Magnus. Were they not glad to be so near home!

Willie Norn hung the token he got from Annie around Mary Foubister's neck. And six weeks after that, they were married.

But fair Annie Norn was never seen or heard of more.

retold by W. TOWRIE and NANCY CUTT

The Dead Man's Nightcap

Iceland

On a farm beside a church there lived, among others, a young boy and a girl. The boy made a habit of scaring the girl, but she had got so used to it that she was never frightened of anything, for if she did see something she thought it was the boy trying to scare her.

One day it so happened that the washing had been done, and that among the things there were many white nightcaps, such as were in fashion then. In the evening the girl was told to fetch in the washing, which was out in the churchyard. She runs out, and begins to pick up the washing. When she has almost finished, she sees a white spectre sitting on one of the graves. She thinks to herself that the lad is planning to scare her, so she runs up and snatches the spectre's cap off (for she thought the boy had taken one of the nightcaps) and says: "Now don't you start trying to scare me this time!"

So she went indoors with the washing; the boy had been indoors the whole time. They started sorting out the washing; there was one nightcap too many now, and it was earthy on the inside. Then the girl was scared.

Next morning the spectre was still sitting on the grave, and people did not know what to do about it, as nobody dared take the cap back, and so they sent word all round the district, asking for advice. There was one old man in the district who declared that it would be impossible to stop something bad coming of it, unless the girl herself took the cap back to the spectre and placed it on its head in silence, and that there ought to be many people there to watch.

The girl was forced to go with the cap and place it on the spectre's head, and so she went, though her heart was not much in it, and she placed the cap on the head of the spectre, and when she had done so she said: "Are you satisfied now?"

But at this the dead man started to his feet, struck her, and said: "Yes! And you, are you satisfied?"

And with these words he plunged down into the grave. The girl fell down at the blow, and when men ran to pick her up, she was already dead. The boy was punished because he used to scare her, for it was considered that the whole unfortunate affair had been his fault, and he gave up scaring people. And that is the end of this tale.

collected by JÓN ÁRNASON
translated by Jacqueline Simpson

ㅂㅂ

The Herd-boy and the Giant

Sweden

ㅂㅂ

There was once a boy who tended goats. One day, when wandering about in the forest, he came to a giant's dwelling, when the giant, hearing a noise and outcry in his neighbourhood, came out to see what was the matter. Now the giant being of a vast stature and fierce aspect, the boy was terrified, and ran away as fast as he was able.

In the evening, when the lad returned with his goats from the pasture, his mother was occupied in curdling. Taking a piece of the new-made cheese, he rolled it in the embers, and put it into his wallet. On the following morning he went, as was his custom, to the pasture, and again approached the giant's abode. When the giant heard the noise of the boy and his goats, he was angry, and rising up, seized a huge piece of granite, which he squeezed in his hand so that the fragments flew about in all directions. The giant then said: "If thou ever comest here again, making an uproar, I will crumple thee as small as I now squeeze this stone." The boy, however, did not allow himself to be frightened, but made a sham also to seize a stone, though he only grasped his cheese that had been rolled in the ashes, and which he pressed till the whey ran out between his fingers, and dripped down on the ground. The boy then said: "If thou dost not take thyself away, and leave me in peace, I will squeeze thee as I now squeeze the water out of this stone." When the giant found that the lad was so strong, he was frightened, and went into his hut. And thus the boy and the giant separated for that time.

On the third day they met again in the forest, and the boy asked whether they should make another trial of strength. The giant consented, and the boy said: "Father, I think it will be a good trial, if one of us can cast your axe so high, that it does not fall down again." The giant thought it would. They now commenced the trial, and the giant threw first. He hurled the axe up with great force, so that it rose high in the air; but let him try as he might, it always fell down again. Then said the boy: "Father, I did not think you had so little strength. Wait a moment, and you shall see a better throw." The boy then swung his arm to and fro, as if to cast with the greater force; but, at the same time, very cleverly let the axe slide down into the wallet that he had on his back. The artifice escaped the notice of the giant, who continued expecting and expecting to see the axe come down again, but no axe appeared. "Now," thought he to himself, "this boy must be amazingly strong, although he appears so little and weak." They then again separated, each going his own way.

Shortly after, the giant and the herd-boy met again, and the giant asked the boy whether he would enter his service. The boy consented, left his goats in the forest, and accompanied the giant to the latter's habitation.

It is related that the giant and the boy set out for the purpose of felling an oak in the forest. When they reached the spot, the giant asked the boy whether he would hold or fell. "I will hold," said the boy, but added that he was unable to reach the top. The giant then grasped the tree and bent it to the ground; but no sooner had the boy taken fast hold of it, than the tree rebounded, and threw the lad high up in the air, so that the giant could hardly follow him with his eyes. The giant stood long wondering in what direction the boy had taken his flight; then taking up his axe, began to hew. In a little while the boy came limping up; for he had escaped with difficulty. The giant asked him why he did not hold; while the boy, who appeared as if nothing had happened, in return, asked the giant whether he would venture to make such a spring as he had just made. The giant answered in the negative, and the boy then said: "If you will not venture to do that, you may both hold and fell yourself." The giant let this answer content him, and felled the oak himself.

When the tree was to be carried home, the giant said to the boy: "If thou wilt bear the top-end, I will bear the root." "No, father," answered the boy, "do you bear the top-end, I am able enough to bear the other." The giant consented, and raised the top end of the oak upon his shoulder; but the boy, who was behind, called to him to poise the tree better by moving it more forwards. The giant did so, and thus got the whole trunk in equilibrium on his shoulder. But the boy leaped up on the tree, and hid himself among the boughs, so that the giant could not see him. The giant now began his march, thinking that the boy was all the while at the other end. When they had thus

proceeded for some distance, the giant thought it was very hard labour, and groaned piteously. "Art thou not yet tired?" said he to the boy. "No, not in the least," answered the boy. "Surely father is not tired with such a trifle." The giant was unwilling to acknowledge that such was the case, and continued on his way. When they reached home, the giant was half-dead from fatigue. He threw the tree down; but the boy had in the meanwhile leaped off, and appeared as if bearing the larger end of the oak. "Art thou not yet tired?" asked the giant. The boy answered: "Oh, father must not think that so little tires me. The trunk does not seem to me heavier than I could have borne by myself."

Another time the giant said: "As soon as it is daylight we will go out and thresh." "Now I," answered the boy, "think it better to thresh before daybreak, before we eat our breakfast." The giant acquiesced, and went and fetched two flails, one of which he took for himself. When they were about to begin threshing, the boy was unable to lift his flail, it was so large and heavy. He therefore took up a stick, and beat on the floor, while the giant threshed. This escaped the giant's notice, and so they continued until daylight. "Now," said the boy, "let us go home to breakfast." "Yes," answered the giant, "for I think we have had a stiff job of it."

Some time after, the giant set his boy to plough, and at the same time, said: "When the dog comes, thou must loose the oxen and put them in the stall to which he will lead the way." The lad promised to do so; but when the oxen were loosed, the giant's dog crept in under the foundation of a building to which there was no door. The giant's object was to ascertain whether his boy were strong enough to lift up the house alone, and place the oxen in their stalls. The boy, after having long considered what was to be done, at length resolved on slaughtering the animals, and casting their carcases in through the window. When he returned home, the giant asked him whether the oxen were in their stalls. "Yes," answered the boy, "I got them in although I divided them."

The giant now began to harbour apprehensions, and consulted with his wife how they should make away with the boy. The crone said: "It is my advice that you take your club and kill him to-night while he is asleep." This the giant thought very sound advice, and promised to follow it. But the boy was on the watch, and listening to their conversation; therefore, when evening came, he laid a churn in the bed, and hid himself behind the door. At midnight the giant rose, seized his club, and beat on the churn so that the cream that was in it was sprinkled over his face. He then went to his wife, and laughing said: "Ha, ha, ha! I have struck him so that his brains flew high up on the wall." The crone was pleased at this intelligence, praised her husband's boldness, and thought they might now sleep in quiet, seeing they had no longer cause to fear the mischievous boy.

Scarcely, however, was it light, when the boy crept out of his hiding-place, went in, and bade the giant-folk good morning. At this apparition the giant was naturally struck with amazement. "What," said he, "art thou not yet dead? I thought I struck thee dead with my club." The boy answered: "I rather believe I felt in the night as if a flea had bitten me."

In the evening, when the giant and his boy were about to sup, the crone placed a large dish of porridge before them. "That would be excellent," said the boy, "if we were to try which could eat the most, father or I." The giant was ready for the trial, and they began to eat with all their might. But the boy was crafty: he had tied his wallet before his chest, and for every spoonful that entered his mouth, he let two fall into the wallet. When the giant had despatched seven bowls of porridge, he had taken his fill, and sat puffing and blowing, and unable to swallow another spoonful; but the boy continued with just as much good will as when he began. The giant asked him how it was, that he who was so little could eat so much. The boy answered: "Father, I will soon show you. When I have eaten as much as I can contain, I slit up my stomach, and then I can take in as much again." Saying these words, he took a knife and ripped up the wallet, so that the porridge ran out. The giant thought this a capital plan, and that he would do the like. But when he stuck the knife in his stomach, the blood began to flow, and the end of the matter was, that it proved his death.

When the giant was dead, the boy took all the chattels that were in the house, and went his way in the night. And so ends the story of the crafty herd-boy and the doltish giant.

retold by BENJAMIN THORPE

Yallery Brown

England

Once upon a time, and a very good time it was, though it wasn't in my time, nor in your time, nor anyone else's time, there was a young lad of eighteen or so named Tom Tiver working on the Hall Farm. One Sunday he was walking across the west field, 'twas a beautiful July night, warm and still and the air was full of little sounds as though the trees and grass were chattering to themselves. And all at once there came a bit ahead of him the pitifullest greetings ever he heard, sob, sobbing, like a bairn spent with fear, and nigh heart-broken; breaking off into a moan and then rising again in a long whimpering wailing that made him feel sick to hark to it. He began to look everywhere for the poor creature. "It must be Sally Bratton's child," he thought to himself; "she was always a flighty thing, and never looked after it. Like as not, she's flaunting about the lanes, and has clean forgot the babby." But though he looked and looked, he could see nought. And presently the whimpering got louder and stronger in the quietness, and he thought he could make out words of some sort. He hearkened with all his ears, and the sorry thing was saying words all mixed up with sobbing—

"Ooh! the stone, the great big stone! ooh! the stone on top!"

Naturally he wondered where the stone might be, and he looked again, and there by the hedge bottom was a great flat stone, nigh buried in the mools, and hid in the cotted* grass and weeds. One of the stones was called the "Strangers' Table". However, down he fell on his knee-bones by that stone, and hearkened again. Clearer than ever, but tired and spent with greeting came the little sobbing

* Matted, tangled.

voice—'Ooh! ooh! the stone, the stone on top." He was gey, and misliking to meddle with the thing, but he couldn't stand the whimpering babby, and he tore like mad at the stone, till he felt it lifting from the mools, and all at once it came with a sough out o' the damp earth and the tangled grass and growing things. And there in the hole lay a tiddy thing on its back, blinking up at the moon and at him. 'Twas no bigger than a year-old baby, but it had long cotted hair and beard, twisted round and round its body so that you couldn't see its clothes; and the hair was all yaller and shining and silky, like a bairn's; but the face of it was old and as if 'twere hundreds of years since 'twas young and smooth. Just a heap of wrinkles, and two bright black eyne in the midst, set in a lot of shining yaller hair; and the skin was the colour of the fresh-turned earth in the spring—brown as brown could be, and its bare hands and feet were brown like the face of it. The greeting had stopped, but the tears were standing on its cheek, and the tiddy thing looked mazed like in the moonshine and the night air.

The creature's eyne got used like to the moonlight, and presently he looked up in Tom's face as bold as ever was; "Tom," says he, "thou'rt a good lad!" as cool as thou can think, says he, "Tom, thou'rt a good lad!" and his voice was soft and high and piping like a little bird twittering.

Tom touched his hat, and began to think what he ought to say. "Houts!" says the thing again, "thou needn't be feared o' me; thou'st done me a better turn than thou know'st, my lad, and I'll do as much for thee." Tom couldn't speak yet, but he thought, "Lord! for sure 'tis a bogle!"

"No!" says he as quick as quick, "I am no bogle, but ye'd best not ask me what I be; anyways I be a good friend o' thine." Tom's very knee-bones struck, for certainly an ordinary body couldn't have known what he'd been thinking to himself, but he looked so kind like, and spoke so fair, that he made bold to get out, a bit quavery like—

"Might I be axing to know your honour's name?"

"H'm," says he, pulling his beard; "as for that"—and he thought a bit—"aye so," he went on at last, "Yallery Brown thou mayst call me, Yallery Brown; 'tis my nature seest thou, and as for a name 'twill do as any other. Yallery Brown, Tom, Yallery Brown's thy friend, my lad."

"Thankee, master," says Tom, quite meek like.

"And now," he says, "I'm in a hurry tonight, but tell me quick, what'll I do for thee? Wilt have a wife? I can give thee the finest lass in the town. Wilt be rich? I'll give thee gold as much as thou can carry. Or wilt have help wi' thy work? Only say the word."

Tom scratched his head. "Well, as for a wife, I have no hankering after such; they're but bothersome bodies, and I have women folk at home as'll mend my clouts; and for gold that's as may be, but for work, there, I can't abide work, and if thou'lt give me a helpin' hand in it I'll thank—"

"Stop," says he, quick as lightning, "I'll help thee and welcome, but if ever thou sayest that to me—if ever thou thankest me, see'st thou, thou'lt never see me more. Mind that now; I want no thanks, I'll have no thanks"; and he stampt his tiddy foot on the earth and looked as wicked as a raging bull.

"Mind that now, great lump that thou be," he went on, calming down a bit, "and if ever thou need'st help, or get'st into trouble, call on me and just say, 'Yallery Brown, come from the mools, I want thee!' and I'll be wi' thee at once; and now," says he, picking a dandelion puff, "good night to thee", and he blowed it up, and it all came into Tom's eyne and ears. Soon as Tom could see again the tiddy creature was gone, and but for the stone on end and the hole at his feet, he'd have thought he'd been dreaming.

Well, Tom went home and to bed; and by the morning he'd nigh forgot all about it. But when he went to the work, there was none to do! All was done already, the horses seen to, the stables cleaned out, everything in its proper place, and he'd nothing to do but sit with his hands in his pockets. And so it went on day after day, all the work done by Yallery Brown, and better done, too, than he could have done it himself. And if the master gave him more work, he sat down, and the work did itself, the singeing irons, or the broom, or what not, set to, and with ne'er a hand put to it would get through in no time. For he never saw Yallery Brown in daylight; only in the darklins he saw him hopping about, like a Will-o-th'-wyke without his lanthorn.

At first 'twas mighty fine for Tom; he'd nought to do and good pay for it; but by and by things began to grow vicey-varsy. If the work was done for Tom, 'twas undone for the other lads; if his buckets were filled, theirs were upset; if his tools were sharpened, theirs were blunted and spoiled; if his horses were clean as daisies, theirs were splashed with muck, and so on; day in and day out, 'twas the same. And the lads saw Yallery Brown flitting about o' nights, and they saw the things working without hands o' days, and they saw that Tom's work was done for him, and theirs undone for them; and naturally they begun to look shy on him, and they wouldn't speak or come nigh

him, and they carried tales to the master and so things went from bad
to worse.

For Tom could do nothing himself; the brooms wouldn't stay in
his hand, the plough ran away from him, the hoe kept out of his grip.
He thought that he'd do his own work after all, so that Yallery Brown
would leave him and his neighbours alone. But he couldn't—true as
death he couldn't. He could only sit by and look on, and have the cold
shoulder turned on him, while the unnatural thing was meddling
with the others, and working for him.

At last, things got so bad that the master gave Tom the sack, and if
he hadn't, all the rest of the lads would have sacked him, for they
swore they'd not stay on the same garth with Tom. Well, naturally
Tom felt bad; 'twas a very good place, and good pay too; and he was
fair mad with Yallery Brown, as'd got him into such a trouble.
So Tom shook his fist in the air and called out as loud as he
could, "Yallery Brown, come from the mools; thou scamp, I
want thee!"

You'll scarce believe it, but he'd hardly brought out the words but
he felt something tweaking his leg behind, while he jumped with the
smart of it; and soon as he looked down, there was the tiddy thing,
with his shining hair, and wrinkled face, and wicked glinting black
eyne.

Tom was in a fine rage, and he would have liked to have kicked
him, but 'twas no good, there wasn't enough of it to get his boot
against; but he said, "Look here, master, I'll thank thee to leave me
alone after this, dost hear? I want none of thy help, and I'll have
nought more to do with thee—see now."

The horrid thing broke into a screeching laugh, and pointed its
brown finger at Tom. "Ho, ho, Tom!" says he. "Thou'st thanked
me, my lad, and I told thee not, I told thee not!"

"I don't want thy help, I tell thee," Tom yelled at him—"I only
want never to see thee again, and to have nought more to do with
'ee—thou can go."

The thing only laughed and screeched and mocked, as long as Tom
went on swearing, but so soon as his breath gave out—

"Tom, my lad," he said with a grin, "I'll tell'ee summat, Tom.
True's true. I'll never help thee again, and call as thou wilt, thou'lt
never see me after today; but I never said that I'd leave thee alone,
Tom, and I never will, my lad! I was nice and safe under the stone,
Tom, and could do no harm; but thou let me out thyself, and thou
can't put me back again! I would have been thy friend and worked for
thee if thou had been wise; but since thou bee'st no more than a born

fool I'll give 'ee no more than a born fool's luck; and when all goes vicey-varsy, and everything agee—thou'lt mind that it's Yallery Brown's doing though m'appen thou doesn't see him. Mark my words, will 'ee?"

And he began to sing, dancing round Tom, like a bairn with his yellow hair, but looking older than ever with his grinning wrinkled bit of a face:

> *"Work as thou will*
> *Thou'lt never do well;*
> *Work as thou mayst*
> *Thou'lt never gain grist;*
> *For harm and mischance and Yallery Brown*
> *Thou'st let out thyself from under the stone."*

Tom could never rightly mind what he said next. 'Twas all cussing and calling down misfortune on him; but he was so mazed in fright that he could only stand there shaking all over, and staring down at the horrid thing; and if he'd gone on long, Tom would have tumbled down in a fit. But by and by, his yaller shining hair rose up in the air, and wrapt itself round him till he looked for all the world like a great dandelion puff; and it floated away on the wind over the wall and out o' sight, with a parting skirl of wicked voice and sneering laugh.

And did it come true, sayst thou? My word! but it did, sure as death! He worked here and he worked there, and turned his hand to this and to that, but it always went agee, and 'twas all Yallery Brown's doing. And the children died, and the crops rotted—the beasts never fatted, and nothing ever did well with him; and till he was dead and buried, and m'appen even afterwards, there was no end to Yallery Brown's spite at him; day in and day out he used to hear him saying—

> *"Work as thou wilt*
> *Thou'lt never do well;*
> *Work as thou mayst*
> *Thou'lt never gain grist;*
> *For harm and mischance and Yallery Brown*
> *Thou'st let out thyself from under the stone."*

retold by JOSEPH JACOBS

The Black Bull of Norroway
Scotland

In Norroway, langsyne, there lived a certain lady, and she had three
dochters.* The auldest o' them said to her mither: "Mither, bake me
a bannock, and roast me a collop,† for I'm gaun awa' to seek my
fortune." Her mither did sae; and the dochter gaed awa' to an auld
witch washerwife and telled her purpose. The auld wife bade her stay
that day, and gang and look out o' her back door, and see what she
could see. She saw nocht the first day. The second day she did the
same, and saw nocht. On the third day she looked again, and saw a
coach-and-six coming alang the road. She ran in and telled the auld
wife what she saw. "Aweel," quo' the auld wife, "yon's for you." Sae
they took her into the coach, and galloped aff.

The second dochter next says to her mither: "Mither, bake me a
bannock, and roast me a collop, for I'm awa' to seek my fortune." Her
mither did sae; and awa' she gaed to the auld wife, as her sister had
dune. On the third day she looked out o' the back door, and saw a
coach-and-four coming along the road. "Aweel," quo' the auld wife,
"yon's for you." Sae they took her in, and aff they set.

The third dochter says to her mither: "Mither, bake me a bannock, and roast me a collop, for I'm awa' to seek my fortune." Her
mither did sae; and awa' she gaed to the auld witch-wife. She bade
her look out o' her back door, and see what she could see. She did sae;
and when she came back said she saw nocht. The second day she did
the same, and saw nocht. The third day she looked again, and on
coming back said to the auld wife she saw nocht but a muckle Black
Bull coming roaring along the road. "Aweel," quo' the auld wife,
"yon's for you." On hearing this she was next to distracted wi' grief

* Daughters.
† Minced meat.

and terror; but she was lifted up and set on his back, and awa' they
went.

Aye they travelled, and on they travelled, till the lady grew faint
wi' hunger. "Eat out o' my right lug'"* says the Black Bull, "and
drink out o' my left lug, and set by your leavings." Sae she did as he
said, and was wonderfully refreshed. And lang they gaed, and sair
they rade, till they came in sight o' a very big and bonny castle.
"Yonder we maun be this night," quo' the bull; "for my auld† brither
lives yonder"; and presently they were at the place. They lifted her
aff his back, and took her in, and sent him away to a park for the
night. In the morning, when they brought the bull hame, they took
the lady into a fine shining parlour, and gave her a beautiful apple,
telling her no to break it till she was in the greatest strait ever mortal
was in in the world, and that wad bring her out o't. Again she was
lifted on the bull's back, and after she had ridden far, and farer than I
can tell, they came in sight o' a far bonnier castle, and far farther awa'
than the last. Says the bull till her: "Yonder we maun be the night,
for my second brither lives yonder"; and they were at the place
directly. They lifted her down and took her in, and sent the bull to
the field for the night. In the morning they took the lady into a fine
and rich room, and gave her the finest pear she had ever seen, bidding
her no to break it till she was in the greatest strait ever mortal could be
in, and that wad get her out o't. Again she was lifted and set on his
back, and awa' they went. And lang they gaed, and sair they rade, till
they came in sight o' the far biggest castle, and far farthest aff, they
had yet seen. "We maun be yonder the night," says the bull, "for my
young brither lives yonder"; and they were there directly. They
lifted her down, took her in, and sent the bull to the field for the
night. In the morning they took her into a room, the finest of a', and
gied her a plum, telling her no to break it till she was in the greatest
strait mortal could be in, and that wad get her out o't. Presently they
brought hame the bull, set the lady on his back, and awa' they went.

And aye they gaed, and on they rade, till they came to a dark and
ugsome glen, where they stopped, and the lady lighted down. Says
the bull to her: "Here ye maun stay till I gang and fight the deil. Ye
maun seat yoursel' on that stane, and move neither hand nor fit‡ till I
come back, else I'll never find ye again. And if everything round
about ye turns blue I hae beaten the deil; but should a' things turn red
he'll hae conquered me." She set hersel' down on the stane, and by
and by a' round her turned blue. O'ercome wi' joy, she lifted the ae fit

* Ear.
† Eldest.   ‡ Foot.

and crossed it owre the ither, sae glad was she that her companion was victorious. The bull returned and sought for but never could find her.

Lang she sat, and aye she grat, till she wearied. At last she rase and gaed awa', she kendna whaur till.* On she wandered till she came to a great hill o' glass, that she tried a' she could to climb, but wasna able. Round the bottom o' the hill she gaed, sabbing and seeking a passage owre, till at last she came to a smith's house; and the smith promised, if she wad serve him seven years, he wad make her iron shoon, wherewi' she could climb owre the glassy hill. At seven years' end she got her iron shoon, clamb the glassy hill, and chanced to come to the auld washerwife's habitation. There she was telied of a gallant young knight that had given in some bluidy sarks† to wash, and whaever washed thae sarks was to be his wife. The auld wife had washed till she was tired, and then she set to her dochter, and baith washed, and they washed, and they better washed, in hopes of getting the young knight; but a' they could do they couldna bring out a stain. At length they set the stranger damosel to wark; and whenever she began the stains came out pure and clean, but the auld wife made the knight believe it was her dochter had washed the sarks. So the knight and the eldest dochter were to be married, and the stranger damosel was distracted at the thought of it, for she was deeply in love wi' him. So she bethought her of her apple, and breaking it, found it filled with gold and precious jewellery, the richest she had ever seen. "All these," she said to the eldest dochter, "I will give you, on condition that you put off your marriage for ae day, and allow me to go into his room alone at night." So the lady consented; but meanwhile the auld wife had prepared a sleeping-drink, and given it to the knight, wha drank it, and never wakened till next morning. The leelang night the damosel sabbed and sang:

> *"Seven lang years I served for thee,*
> *The glassy hill I clamb for thee,*
> *The bluidy shirt I wrang for thee;*
> *And wilt thou no wauken and turn to me?"*

Next day she kentna what to do for grief. She then brak the pear, and found it filled wi' jewellery far richer than the contents o' the apple. Wi' thae jewels she bargained for permission to be a second night in the young knight's chamber; but the auld wife gied him

* She didn't know where to.   † Shirts.

anither sleeping-drink, and he again sleepit till morning. A' night she kept sighing and singing as before:

> *"Seven lang years I served for thee,*
> *The glassy hill I clamb for thee,*
> *The bluidy shirt I wrang for thee;*
> *And wilt thou no wauken and turn to me?"*

Still he sleepit, and she nearly lost hope a'thegeither. But that day when he was out at the hunting, somebody asked him what noise and moaning was yon they heard all last night in his bedchamber. He said he heardna ony noise. But they assured him there was sae; and he resolved to keep waking that night to try what he could hear. That being the third night, and the damosel being between hope and despair, she brak her plum, and it held far the richest jewellery of the three. She bargained as before; and the auld wife, as before, took in the sleeping-drink to the young knight's chamber; but he telled her he couldna drink it that night without sweetening. And when she gaed awa' for some honey to sweeten it wi', he poured out the drink, and sae made the auld wife think he had drunk it. They a' went to bed again, and the damosel began, as before, singing:

> *"Seven lang years I served for thee,*
> *The glassy hill I clamb for thee,*
> *The bluidy shirt I wrang for thee;*
> *And wilt thou no wauken and turn to me?"*

He heard, and turned to her. And she telled him a' that had befa'en her, and he telled her a' that had happened to him. And he caused the auld washerwife and her dochter to be burnt. And they were married, and he and she are living happy till this day, for aught I ken.

retold by ANDREW LANG

The Bold Soldier of Antwerp
Flanders

There was in former days a house in the Little Market at Antwerp that had four stories, and was as beautiful as a royal palace; but no one would live in it because it was haunted. At the stroke of twelve there came a spectre, that ran up and down the stairs; and when it struck one, it would place itself behind the street-door, and begin to howl so horribly that everyone felt pity for it. But no one had courage enough to enter the house, which thus continued empty, although the ghost every night cried: "Release my soul! Release my soul!"

This had continued a long while, when an old soldier from the wars came to the city, who, on hearing people speak of the house, said he would sleep a night in it, if a hundred guilders were given him beforehand. The landlord wondered at this, but the soldier said he feared neither devil nor goblin; for what God protects is well protected. The landlord then said: "Give me thy hand as a pledge, and tell me with what I must provide thee." "Give me," said the soldier, "a good supply of wood cut small, a dozen bottles of wine, a bottle of brandy, and a pot full of dough, together with a good pan, that I may bake my cakes." "That thou shalt have," answered the landlord; and when the soldier had all he required, he went with it at nightfall into the house.

Having struck a light, he carried all his gear into an apartment on the first story, in which there still remained a table and two chairs, and then made a large fire on the hearth, by which he placed his dough, that it might rise a little. He next broke the necks off his bottles, and so did not long continue altogether sober, though he well knew what he said and did. Thirst being now succeeded by hunger, he took his pan, set it on the fire, and threw into it a good ladleful of dough. The cake promised well, smelt most temptingly, was already brown on one side, and the soldier was in the act of turning it, when something suddenly fell down the chimney into the pan, and the cake was in the ashes!

The soldier was not a little angry at this disaster, but reconciled himself to his fate and filled the pan anew. While the cake was baking, he looked at what had fallen down the chimney and found it was an arm-bone. At this the brave warrior began to laugh, and said: "You want to frighten me, but you won't do it with your horse's bone." He then seized the pan, to take out the cake, preferring to eat it half baked rather than undergo a second disappointment; but in the same instant a rattling was heard in the chimney, a number of bones fell into the pan, and the cake into the ashes.

"Now, by Jove," said he, "that is too bad. They ought to let me be quiet, for I am hungry. To pitch the whole back-bone of a colt into my pan!" But he was grievously mistaken, for it was the back-bone of a human being. Highly enraged he seized the bones and dashed them with such violence against the wall that they flew in pieces. Out of humour he again sat down by the pan and made several attempts to bake his cake, but every time down fell one or other bone, and, by way of conclusion, a skull, which the soldier hurled as far as he could send it.

"Now the sport will be at an end," said he, and began again to bake, and this time without interruption, so that he had a good dishful of cakes on the table, and had already sat down and was eating comfortably, when the clock struck. He counted; it was twelve. In the same instant he looked up, and saw that in the corner facing him the bones had united and stood there as a hideous skeleton with a white linen over its shoulders. The soldier rubbed his eyes, thinking it a dream, but seeing that it was a real skeleton, he called to it merrily: "Ha Mr Death! how goes it? you are uncommonly thin. But come and eat and drink with me, provided cake and wine will not fall through your body." The skeleton made no answer, but merely pointed with its finger. "Well, speak then, if you are from God," said he laughing; "but if from the devil, make yourself scarce." The skeleton continued pointing, but said nothing, and the soldier growing tired of this, ate on leisurely, taking no further notice of its movements. It now struck half-past twelve, and the skeleton striding out of its corner, approached the table. "Ah," cried the soldier, "say what you want, but keep at a distance, else we are no longer friends." The skeleton then stretching forth its hands, touched that of the soldier and burned a hole in it. "Hui, the devil!" cried he, "what's this?" at the same time snatching up an empty bottle and hurling it at the skeleton; but it flew in vacant space. He was now in a towering passion, and would thrust the spectre out, but he grasped the empty air, the skeleton constantly making signs and pointing towards the door.

The soldier at length growing weary of this dumb show, took up the light and said: "Well, I'll go with you, do you only go first."

The skeleton went first as far as the stairs, and made a sign to the soldier that he should go down; but he was prudent enough not to do so, saying: "Go you first, always first; you shall not break my neck." They thus descended into a passage, in which lay a heavy stone, having an iron ring in it. The ghost made a sign to him to raise the stone, but he laughed and said: "If you want to lift up the stone, you must do it yourself." The ghost did so, and the soldier then saw that there was a great hole beneath it, in which stood three iron pots. "Do you see that money?" said the skeleton. "Aha, countryman, you speak Flemish," cried the soldier, highly delighted, "that's capital. Yes, I see something that looks like a ten-guilder piece."

The ghost now drew up the three pots and said: "This is money which I concealed before my death." "So," said the soldier, "you are dead then?" The ghost continued without answering, "I had to burn in hell as long as the money was not found. You have released me from hell." "A pretty fellow you!" said the soldier; "in gratitude for the service, you have burnt my hand." "I shall burn no more," said the ghost laughing; "just feel my hand now, it's quite cold." But the other drawing back his hand, cried: "Much obliged all the same, no ceremony; I know you birds." "Now I beseech you to bestow one of the pots on the poor, to give one to the church that masses may be said for my soul, and"—"This is an awkward business," exclaimed the soldier, "I am not your lackey. But what were you going to say?" "The third pot is for you," whispered the ghost. And the soldier leaped and danced and fell into the hole and his light with him, so that he sat in the dark. "Ho spritekin," cried he, "give me a lift out!" But the ghost had vanished, and he had to scramble out as well as he could. When he again found himself safe on the ground, he felt for his candle and for the stairs, went up, and lay down to sleep.

On the following day he did as the ghost had directed, gave one pot to the poor, another to the church, and found so much in the third, that he became a very rich man, rode every day in a coach, and went every day to the tavern.

retold by BENJAMIN THORPE

The Ghost and the Money-chest

Iceland

There was once a landlord of a church-farm in the north. He was married and a man of great wealth, but much given to hoarding, so that men were convinced that he must possess a large sum of money. His wife was a good woman and very charitable, but she had little influence over her miserly husband.

One winter the farmer fell ill, and died soon afterwards, and his body was laid out and buried. The estate was now put in order, but no money was found. The widow was asked if she knew of any, but answered not so much as a single shilling, and since men knew nothing but good of her, her word was not questioned. It was the guess of many that he must have buried the money, as was indeed later found to have been the case.

As the winter advanced, people at the church-farm became aware of haunting, and it was the general view that the farmer was walking on account of his hidden money. The haunting increased to such a degree that most of the work-people decided to leave in the spring, and the widow began making preparations to sell the property.

Time passed till the flitting-days arrived. Then a labourer came to the widow and asked to be hired, and she took him. After he had been there a while, however, he too became aware of a considerable amount of haunting. Once he asked his mistress whether her late husband had not possessed a large quantity of money, but as before she replied that she knew nothing of it.

The days now passed until it was market time. The hired man went to market, and among other things he bought a quantity of sheet iron and a length of white linen. And when he got home, he had a shroud sewn of the linen, while from the sheet-iron he made himself a breastplate and iron gloves, for he was a skilful smith.

Time passed, until once more the days grew shorter and the nights dark. Then one evening, when all were asleep, the hired man put on the breastplate and iron gloves, and then the shroud over all, and went out into the churchyard. Going close to the farmer's grave, he walked back and forth there, playing with a silver piece in the palm of his hand.

It was not long before a ghost rose up from the farmer's grave, and coming quickly to the hired man, it asked, "Are you one of us?"

"Yes," answered the hired man.

"Let me feel you," said the ghost.

The hired man now reached out a hand and the ghost felt how cold it was. It said, "True enough, you are a ghost, too. Why are you walking?"

"To play with my silver piece," replied the other.

At this, the ghost hopped over the churchyard wall, and the hired man after it. They went on until they came to the edge of the homefield. Then the ghost turned over a hummock and pulled up its money-chest, and they took to playing with the money. This went on all night, but when dawn began to approach the ghost would have put the money away. Then the other said that he wanted to take a look at the small change, and he began playing with it and scattering it about all over again. Then the ghost said, "I am not sure you are a ghost."

"Oh yes I am," said the other. "Feel for yourself"—and he held out the other hand.

"True enough," said the ghost, and it now began to collect all the money together again. But still the hired man kept throwing it hither and thither.

The ghost now became angry and said that he must be a living man and meant to cheat it, but he denied this. The ghost then clutched him by the chest, and felt the iron plate on him, and how cold it was.

"What you say is true; you are the same as I am," said the ghost. And once again it began to collect its money together. The hired man now dared not but let it have its way, and said, "Let me put my silver piece with your money."

"Certainly," said the ghost, and it now replaced the hummock so that nothing could be seen. After this they returned to the churchyard.

"Where is your hole?" asked the ghost.

"On the other side of the church," replied the other.

"You go into yours first," said the ghost.

"No," said the hired man, "you go first."

They continued to argue about this until dawn. Then the ghost jumped into its grave, while the hired man returned to the farm-house.

He now filled a cask with water and placed it under the platform. Into this he put his garments of the night and also went out and fetched the money-chest, which he put in as well.

The day passed and evening came, and all went to bed. The hired man slept by the door, and the night was not far advanced when the ghost came in, sniffing and snuffing all about, and struck a mighty blow on the edge of the platform, after which it went out, the hired man following.

Men say that he now dealt in such wise with the farmer's grave that the ghost was never seen again.

He had put his garments and the money-chest in water so that the ghost should not be able to smell earth on them.

The hired man married the widow, and they lived together for many years.

And so ends this story.

collected by JÓN ÁRNASON and MAGNÚS GRÍMSSON
translated by Alan Boucher

ᒲᒲᒲᒲᒲᒲᒲᒲᒲᒲᒲᒲᒲᒲᒲᒲᒲᒲᒲᒲ ᒲᒲᒲᒲᒲᒲᒲᒲᒲᒲᒲᒲᒲᒲᒲᒲᒲᒲᒲᒲᒲᒲ

The Water-sprite and the Bear
Germany

ᒲᒲᒲᒲᒲᒲᒲᒲᒲᒲᒲᒲᒲᒲᒲᒲᒲᒲᒲᒲ ᒲᒲᒲᒲᒲᒲᒲᒲᒲᒲᒲᒲᒲᒲᒲᒲᒲᒲᒲᒲᒲ

In a mill beside a stream, a short way from a village, lived a miller. He was a cheerful, good-natured man, and would have been contented enough with his lot had it not been for one misfortune. In the stream close by the mill lived a water-sprite, a sly, ugly creature with dank hair like water-weeds, sharp, pointed teeth and flat, webbed feet.

At first it was bad enough when the water-sprite's head would suddenly appear above the water and he would look inquisitively as anyone passed by; but it was worse when he began to climb on to the bank of the stream and sit there, showing his long teeth in a thoughtful grin and watching with his unblinking, pebble-like eyes the miller or his wife, the serving-wench or the boy who helped in the mill.

"He gives me the creeps," said the miller's wife, "sitting there like that." And the boy said, "He is ugly, and no mistake." But the serving-wench just gave a scream whenever she caught sight of him, picked up her skirts and ran.

Yet all that was nothing to what came later. The miller had had little to grumble about so far. But one day the water-sprite padded up the steps to the mill, put his head round the door, said, "Good morning, miller," in his wet voice and came in and settled himself comfortably on the floor in a corner by the hearth.

The miller was not one to grudge a warm, dry corner to anyone, not even to a water-sprite—the last kind of creature, surely, whom one would expect to want such a thing—but the water-sprite took to coming into the mill whenever it pleased him, at any hour of the day or night, and prowling around for all the world as though it were his own place, so that, just when one least expected him, there he would be: under the table at supper time, waiting in the kitchen the first thing in the morning, padding behind one on his silent feet when one

had supposed oneself to be alone, or appearing suddenly at a dark
turn of the stairs just as one was going to bed. Or perhaps the very
worst of all was when, after an evening in which he had—most
happily—failed to appear at all, he would be found curled up asleep
in the middle of the bed, lying on a patch of damp bedclothes, for, of
course, he always dripped stream water wherever he went.

In a few weeks he was quite at home in the mill, and one could be
sure of meeting him there at least once every day. By this time the
serving-wench had left—running all the way home to the village one
night after finding the water-sprite on the stairs in the dark—and her
place had been taken by no fewer than three others, each of whom
had, in turn, quickly followed her example, and the miller's wife was
having to do all her own work.

One evening, the water-sprite showed great interest while the
miller's wife was cooking the supper, coming quite close and sniffing
at the roasting meat. The next morning he arrived at breakfast time,
carrying a fish on the end of a stick. He sat himself down by the
hearth and broiled his fish over the fire. When it was cooked, he
tasted it cautiously, liked what he tasted and ate it up in two bites.
After that he always cooked his meals at the hearth, four or five fish at
breakfast and supper, and scrunched them up, heads and tails and
bones and all, with his long teeth; watching the miller and his wife
thoughtfully as he did so, in a manner which they found most
disconcerting. It quite put them off their own meals.

Another pretty trick of his was to set the mill wheel racing in the
middle of the night, so that the miller and his wife would wake up in a
fright, and the miller would have to get up and go to see what was the
matter.

It was, of course, inevitable, with such a state of affairs, that there
should come a day when the miller found himself alone in the mill.
Not a single girl from the village would come to work for him, his
boy's father had found the lad another master, and his wife had gone
home to her mother. So the miller was all alone—all alone, that is,
save for the water-sprite. But because the mill was his livelihood and
had been his home as well for all his life, he had to stay on, in
company with the water-sprite; and little comfort he found in such a
companion.

One evening, just after dark, a bearward knocked on the door of
the mill and asked lodging for the night. He was on his way from one
village to another with his dancing bear. The miller sighed, for he
dearly liked a good evening's talk and he saw little enough of other
folk these days, and the bearward looked a cheerful fellow with a

merry grin and a bright eye, a man, indeed, after the miller's own heart.

"It is unlike me to be inhospitable," said the miller. "Not so long ago I never dreamt there would come a day when I would turn a stranger from my door at night. The village is only a few miles on, my friend, you had best go there, to the inn." And he told the bearward about the water-sprite. "It is all I can do, to stay here myself," he said. "A hundred times a week I tell myself, 'Tomorrow I shall lock the door and throw the key in the stream and go.' But I always manage just one day more. Yet one cannot expect a stranger to put up with it."

"I am not afraid of a water-sprite," said the bearward with a chuckle. "But I have walked a long way today, and I have no mind to walk even a few miles more. I am tired, and so is Braun here." He jerked a thumb over his shoulder towards the shaggy brown bear on the end of a chain.

"Very well," said the miller, "come in, and most welcome you will be. But never say I did not warn you." He stood aside to let the bearward through. "You had best bring your bear in with you, you never know what may happen to him if you leave him in the barn."

The bearward laughed. "Braun can take care of himself. He would make short work of any water-sprite, I warrant. Just you let us have a sight of this plague of yours and we may be able to do you a service, Braun and I."

The water-sprite had already had his supper and gone back to the stream, so the two men had a pleasant evening together, chatting of this and that, and since the water-sprite did not appear again before they went to bed, to the miller it seemed quite like old times, and he began to feel more cheerful than he had felt for months.

The miller and his guest shared the big bedroom, with the bear curled up on the floor beside the bed; and there was no sign of the water-sprite all night.

They got up early in the morning and went down to the kitchen for their breakfast, the bear coming after them. But, early as they were, the water-sprite was earlier. There he was, sitting by the hearth, the embers raked together to make a good fire for him to cook his breakfast on, and four broiled fishes laid out on the floor beside him in a row, ready for him to eat when he had cooked the fifth.

The miller's face fell, and the morning suddenly seemed not so bright and pleasant after all. "There he is," he whispered miserably.

The water-sprite looked up, showed his teeth and, "Good morning, miller," he said. He gave one glance at the stranger, saw nothing to interest him there, and went on with the cooking of his last fish.

The bearward watched him for a moment, then he turned to the miller, winked, and called back over his shoulder, "Come on, Braun, here is your breakfast for you. Look, good fish." He pointed, gave the bear a push, and the bear ambled towards the hearth, sniffed at the fishes laid out on the floor, liked what it smelt, picked one up and swallowed it in one bite—one bite more quickly than the water-sprite could have managed. Before the water-sprite realized what was happening, the bear had taken a second helping; but before it could manage a third, the water-sprite had jumped to his feet, quite furious, and was shaking his fists at the bear. "Away with you! Away with you, you thieving creature!"

The bear sat up and looked at the water-sprite, but made no attempt to go away. Instead, after a moment, it made a move to take the third fish.

"My fish! My fish!" screamed the water-sprite, beside himself with rage. And he rushed at the bear to drive it away.

The bear put out a great paw and clouted the water-sprite, who shrieked and turned tail, making for the mill door and his stream as fast as he could, followed by the growling bear. At the door the bear turned and came back for the remaining three fishes, which it ate happily by the fire; while the miller, delighted with the way things had turned out, made the breakfast.

The bearward laughed loudly. "Well," he said, "did I or did I not tell you that Braun would make short work of any water-sprite?"

After breakfast the bearward went on his way to the village and the miller began his work, feeling happier than he had felt for a very long time. In fact, he felt so happy that he sang at his work, a thing he had long forgotten to do.

All that day the water-sprite never showed himself near the mill, and it was the same the next day, and the next, for nearly a week; and the miller was feeling on top of the world and thinking of taking a day off from work the very next morning and going over to his wife's mother's house to tell his wife to come home, when, coming whistling into the kitchen for supper, he saw the water-sprite sitting by the hearth cooking his fish.

The miller could have wept. Now it would start all over again, he thought. No wife, no boy to help him, no serving-wench, no peace in the mill ever again.

"Good evening, miller," said the water-sprite, showing his long teeth. But the miller had not even the heart to give him a civil

answer—though he usually did, just in case the water-sprite took offence: one never knew, and it was always best to be on the safe side, with those long teeth.

The miller sat down at the table, too miserable to trouble about getting himself any supper. After a time the water-sprite said, "That big cat of yours with the long claws, miller; I have not seen it for several days. Has it gone away?"

For a moment the miller went on staring at the table top, thinking regretfully of the bear; not even finding the idea of a bear-sized cat amusing, though it would once have made him laugh. Then suddenly his heart gave a great bound, for he was really quite a quick-witted man. He looked up and said, as casually as he could, "Why no! She has just had kittens. You will be seeing her around again soon, and all the seven little ones with her. They are just like their mother, only smaller. But they will soon grow. They will soon grow."

The water-sprite looked at the miller with his round, pebbly eyes even rounder than usual, if that were possible. Then he dropped the fish he was cooking and sprang up. "Is that so? Seven little ones?" he said with a shriek. "Then I am off! Good-bye, miller, you will not be seeing me again." And he was away out of the mill as fast as his flat feet could carry him, and into the water and down the stream and away for good and all.

And the miller never set eyes on him again.

retold by BARBARA LEONIE PICARD

ᒒᒒᒒ

Eiríkur Rescues a Woman from the Otherworld
Iceland

ᒒᒒ

A newly married farmer on the Vestmanna Islands, a young and promising man, lost his wife in this way: One day she got up early, as she often did, while her husband was still in bed; she went as usual to relight the fire, but stayed out of doors longer than she generally did, so that her husband got tired of waiting. So up he gets, and goes and looks for her, and cannot find her anywhere on the farm. Then he goes round various cottages asking news of her, but nobody has seen her that morning. A search party is sent to look for her that day, and on the following days too, but she is not to be found.

Her husband was so distressed by her disappearance that he took to his bed and could neither sleep nor eat; and so time went on, and he grew more and more wretched the longer he lay there. The thing that weighed on him most was not knowing what had killed his wife—for he felt sure she was dead, and very likely in the sea. People thought he would pine away and die, for the more they tried to comfort him, the more heavy-hearted he became.

Finally, a friend of his came to him and said: "Don't you think you might try to get up if I gave you a piece of advice which we could hope might lead to your finding out what has become of your wife?"

"I would willingly try, if I thought I could," said the farmer.

"Then pull yourself together," said the other, "and get up, and get dressed, and eat. Then go to the mainland, go to Selvogur and see Eiríkur the priest at Vogsósar, and ask him to find out what has become of your wife."

The farmer grew a little more cheerful at this, then he dressed and ate, and little by little he pulled himself together till he was strong enough to go over to the mainland; and there is nothing to say of his

journey until he comes to Eiríkur at Vogsósar. Eiríkur is standing at
the door, welcomes him, and asks him his errand, and the farmer
tells him about it.

Eiríkur says: "I don't know what has become of your wife, but stay
here for a few days, if you like, and we'll see what happens."

The farmer accepts. Now two or three days go by, and then
Eiríkur has two grey horses brought up to the house; one was a very
fine beast, the other ugly and thin. Eiríkur has the latter saddled for
himself and the other one for the farmer, and says: "Now we'll go for
a ride along the shore."

The farmer said: "Don't ride that old bag of bones; this one will
carry you better."

Eiríkur pretended not to have heard. So they ride off from the
farmstead, though there was a storm, and heavy rain. When they
came to the mouth of the river, the lean horse lengthened his stride,
and rapidly drew ahead. The farmer followed as best he could, but
Eiríkur soon disappeared in the distance. Still, he went on and on till
he came to the foot of Geitahlíd, to the rocks which mark the
boundary between the districts of Árnes and Gullbringa. Eiríkur is
there, waiting for him, and he has laid a very large book open on the
biggest rock. Not a drop of rain fell on it, and not a page of it shook,
though there was a great wind blowing.

Eiríkur went widdershins round the rock, and muttered something between his teeth, and then he says to the farmer: "Look
carefully whether you see your wife coming."

Now a crowd of people comes out from the rock, and the farmer
walked round and round each one, and he did not find his wife. He
told Eiríkur so, and Eiríkur said to these people: "Go in peace, and
thank you for having come," and they vanished at once.

Eiríkur turned a few pages of his book, and the same thing
happened all over again. He tried a third time, and it was just the
same. When this last group had gone, Eiríkur said: "Was she really
not among any of these bands?"

The farmer said she was not.

Then Eiríkur grew red, and said: "Things are getting difficult, my
good fellow. I have summoned all the Otherworld beings I know of,
whether on the earth, under the earth, or in the sea."

Then he takes a single sheet of parchment from his breast, looks at
it, and says: "Ah, there's still the couple who live inside Hauhlíd
Mountain."

He lays the parchment, unfolded, on the open book, goes widdershins round the rock, and mumbles as before. Then along come a

troll and his wife, carrying a glass cage between them; inside it, the farmer sees his wife.

Eiríkur says to them: "You did wrong to take a man's wife from him. Go back home, and no thanks to you for what you've done. And never do such a thing again!"

At once the trolls depart, but Eiríkur breaks the glass cage, takes the woman out, and remounts his horse with her and his book as well.

The farmer says: "Let me take my wife up behind me; that horse will never carry you both."

Eiríkur answered that that was his own affair, and disappeared in the distance across the lava outcrops to the east. The farmer goes on his way and comes to Vogsósar, where Eiríkur had already arrived, and that night Eiríkur made the woman sleep in his own bed, while he lay on a pallet near the door.

Next morning the farmer prepared to go home again. Eiríkur said: "It's not wise to let your wife go off with you like this; I'll get her safe home for you."

The farmer thanks him. Then the priest mounts the old carthorse, sets the woman on his knee, and sets out. The farmer followed after, but he saw no more of Eiríkur till he reached his own home in the islands, where Eiríkur and the woman had arrived already. That evening the farmer took his wife into his bed, but Eiríkur kept guard over them for three nights running, after which time he said: "I don't suppose many people would have enjoyed keeping guard these three nights, and last night least of all. But your wife will be in no danger from now on."

While Eiríkur was guarding the woman he gave her a drink every morning, and so she got her memory back, which otherwise she would have lost for ever. Then Eiríkur went home again, but first he received fine gifts from the farmer.

collected by JÓN ÁRNASON
translated by Jacqueline Simpson

Mr Miacca

England

Tommy Grimes was sometimes a good boy, and sometimes a bad boy; and when he was a bad boy, he was a very bad boy. Now his mother used to say to him: "Tommy, Tommy, be a good boy, and don't go out of the street, or else Mr Miacca will take you." But still when he was a bad boy he would go out of the street; and one day, sure enough, he had scarcely got round the corner, when Mr Miacca did catch him and popped him into a bag upside down, and took him off to his house.

When Mr Miacca got Tommy inside, he pulled him out of the bag and sat him down, and felt his arms and legs. "You're rather tough," says he; "but you're all I've got for supper, and you'll not taste bad boiled. But body o' me, I've forgot the herbs, and it's bitter you'll taste without herbs. Sally! Here, I say, Sally!" and he called Mrs Miacca.

So Mrs Miacca came out of another room and said: "What d'ye want, my dear?"

"Oh, here's a little boy for supper," said Mr Miacca, "and I've forgot the herbs. Mind him, will ye, while I go for them."

"All right, my love," says Mrs Miacca, and off he goes.

Then Tommy Grimes said to Mrs Miacca: "Does Mr Miacca always have little boys for supper?"

"Mostly, my dear," said Mrs Miacca, "if little boys are bad enough, and get in his way."

"And don't you have anything else but boy-meat? No pudding?" asked Tommy.

"Ah, I loves pudding," says Mrs Miacca. "But it's not often the likes of me gets pudding."

"Why, my mother is making a pudding this very day," said

Tommy Grimes, "and I am sure she'd give you some, if I ask her. Shall I run and get some?"

"Now, that's a thoughtful boy," said Mrs Miacca, "only don't be long and be sure to be back for supper."

So off Tommy pelted, and right glad he was to get off so cheap; and for many a long day he was as good as good could be, and never went round the corner of the street. But he couldn't always be good; and one day he went round the corner, and as luck would have it, he hadn't scarcely got round it when Mr Miacca grabbed him up, popped him in his bag, and took him home.

When he got him there, Mr Miacca dropped him out; and when he saw him, he said: "Ah, you're the youngster that served me and my missus such a shabby trick, leaving us without any supper. Well, you shan't do it again. I'll watch over you myself. Here, get under the sofa, and I'll set on it and watch the pot boil for you."

So poor Tommy Grimes had to creep under the sofa, and Mr Miacca sat on it and waited for the pot to boil. And they waited and they waited, but still the pot didn't boil, till at last Mr Miacca got tired of waiting, and he said: "Here, you under there, I'm not going to wait any longer; put out your leg, and I'll stop your giving us the slip."

So Tommy put out a leg and Mr Miacca got a chopper, and chopped it off, and pops it in the pot.

Suddenly he calls out: "Sally, my dear, Sally!" and nobody answered. So he went into the next room to look out for Mrs Miacca, and while he was there Tommy crept out from under the sofa and ran out of the door. For it was a leg of the sofa that he had put out.

So Tommy Grimes ran home, and he never went round the corner again till he was old enough to go alone.

retold by JOSEPH JACOBS

The Three Sisters who were Entrapped into a Mountain

Norway

There was once an old widow who lived far from any inhabited spot, under a mountain-ridge, with her three daughters. She was so poor that all she possessed was a hen, and this was as dear to her as the apple of her eye; she petted and fondled it from morning till night. But one day it so happened, that the hen was missing. The woman looked everywhere about her room, but the hen was away, and remained away. "Thou must go out and search for our hen," said the woman to her eldest daughter, "for have it back again we must, even if we have to get it out of the mountain." So the daughter went in search of the hen. She went about in all directions, and searched and coaxed, yet no hen could she find; but all at once she heard a voice from a mountain-side—

"The hen trips in the mountain!
The hen trips in the mountain!"

She went naturally to see whence it proceeded; but just as she came to the spot, she fell through a trap-door, far far down into a vault under the earth. Here she walked through many rooms, every one more beautiful than the other; but in the last a great ugly Troll came to her, and asked her if she would be his wife. "No," she answered, she would not on any account, she would go back again directly, and look after her hen which had wandered away. On hearing this, the Troll was so angry, that he seized her and wrung her head off, and then threw her head and body down into a cellar.

The mother in the meantime sat at home expecting and expecting, but no daughter came back. After waiting a long time, and neither hearing nor seeing anything more of her, she said to the second daughter, that she must go out and look after her sister, and at the same time "coax back the hen".

Now the second daughter went out, and it happened to her just as it had to her sister; she looked and looked about, and all at once, she also heard a voice from a mountain-side say:

"The hen trips in the mountain!
The hen trips in the mountain!"

This she thought very strange, and she would go and see whence it proceeded, and so she fell also through the trapdoor, deep deep down into the vault. Here she went through all the rooms, and in the innermost the Troll came to her and asked if she would be his wife. "No," she would not on any account, she would go up again instantly and search for her hen, which had gone astray. Thereupon the Troll was so exasperated that, catching hold of her, he wrung her head off and threw both head and body into the cellar.

When the mother had waited a long time for the other daughter, and no daughter was to be seen or heard of, she said to the youngest: "Now thou must set out and seek after thy sisters. Bad enough it was that the hen strayed away, but worse will it be, if we cannot find thy sisters again, and the hen thou canst also coax back at the same time." So the youngest was now to go out; she went in all directions, and looked and coaxed, but she neither saw the hen nor her sisters. After wandering about for some time, she came at length to the mountain-side and heard the same voice saying:

"The hen trips in the mountain!
The hen trips in the mountain!"

This seemed to her extraordinary, but she would go and see whence it came, and so she also fell through the trapdoor deep deep down into the vault. Here she went through many rooms every one finer than the other; but she was not terrified, and gave herself time to look at this and at that, and then cast her eyes on the trap-door to the cellar; on looking down she immediately saw her two sisters, who lay there dead. Just as she had shut the trap-door again, the Troll came to her. "Wilt thou be my wife?" asked the Troll. "Yes, willingly," said the girl, for she saw well enough how it had fared with her sisters. When the Troll heard this, he gave her splendid clothes, the most beautiful she could wish for, and everything she desired, so delighted was he that somebody would be his mate.

When she had been there some time, she was one day more sad and silent than usual; whereupon the Troll asked her what it was that grieved her. "Oh!" answered she, "it is because I cannot go home again to my mother, I am sure she both hungers and thirsts, and she has no one with her." "Thou canst not be allowed to go to her," said the Troll, "but put some food in a sack, and I will carry it to her." For this she thanked him, and would do so, she said; but at the bottom of the sack she stuffed in a great deal of gold and silver, and then laid a little food on the top, telling the Troll the sack was ready, but that he must on no account look into it; and he promised that he would not. As soon as the Troll was gone, she watched him through a little hole there was in the door. When he had carried it some way, he said: "This sack is so heavy, I will see what is in it," and was just about to untie the strings, when the girl cried out: "I see you, I see you." "What sharp eyes thou hast got in thy head," said the Troll, and durst not repeat the attempt. On reaching the place where the widow dwelt, he threw the sack in through the door of the room, saying: "There's food for thee from thy daughter, she wants for nothing."

When the young girl had been for some time in the mountain, it happened one day that a goat fell through the trap-door. "Who sent for thee, thou long-bearded beast!" said the Troll, and fell into a violent passion; so, seizing the goat, he wrung its head off, and threw it into the cellar. "Oh! why did you do that?" said the girl; "he might have been some amusement to me down here." "Thou needst not put on such a fast-day face," said the Troll, "I can soon put life into the goat again." Saying this he took a flask, which hung against the wall, set the goat's head on again, rubbed it with what was in the flask, and the animal was as sound as ever. "Ha, ha!" thought the girl, "that flask is worth something." When she had been some time longer with the Troll, and he was one day gone out, she took the eldest of her sisters, set her head on, and rubbed her with what was in the flask, just as she had seen the Troll do with the goat, and her sister came instantly to life again. The girl then put her into a sack with a little food at the top; and as soon as the Troll came home, she said to him: "Dear friend, you must go again to my mother, and carry her a little food; I am sure she both hungers and thirsts, poor thing! and she is so lonely; but do not look into the sack." He promised to take the sack, and also that he would not look into it. When he had gone some distance, he thought the sack very heavy, and going on a little further, he said: "This sack is so heavy, I must see what is in it; for of whatever her eyes may be made, I am sure she can't see me now." But just as he was going to untie the sack, the girl who was in it cried out: "I can see you, I can see you." "What sharp eyes thou must have in thy head," said the Troll; for he thought it was the girl in the mountain that spoke, and therefore did not dare to look again, but carried it as fast as he could to the mother; and when he came to the door, he threw it inside, saying: "There is some food for thee from thy daughter, she wants for nothing."

Some time after this the girl in the mountain performed a like operation on her second sister; she set her head on again, rubbed her with what was in the flask, and put her into a sack; but this time she put as much gold and silver into the sack as it would hold, and only a very little food on the top. "Dear friend," said she to the Troll, "you must go home again to my mother with a little more food, but do not look into the sack." The Troll was quite willing to please her, and promised he would not look into the sack. But when he had gone a good way, the sack was so insufferably heavy that he was obliged to sit down and rest awhile, being quite unable to carry it any farther; so he thought he would untie the string and look into it; but the girl in the sack called out: "I can see you. I can see you!" "Then thou must have sharp eyes indeed, in thy head," said the Troll quite frightened, and taking up the sack, made all the haste he could to the mother's. When he came to the door of the room, he threw it in, saying: "There is some food from thy daughter for thee, she is in want of nothing."

When the young girl had been some time longer in the mountain, the Troll having occasion one day to go out, she pretended to be ill and sick, and complained. "It is of no use that you come home before twelve o'clock," said she to the Troll, "for I feel so sick and ill that I cannot get the dinner ready before that time"; so the Troll promised he would not come back.

When the Troll was gone she stuffed her clothes out with straw, and set the straw girl in the chimney-corner with a ladle in her hand, so that she looked exactly as if she were standing there herself. She then stole home clandestinely, and took with her a gamekeeper, whom she met, to be at home with her mother. When the clock struck twelve the Troll returned. "Give me something to eat," said he to the straw girl; but she made him no answer.

"Give me something to eat, I say," said the Troll again; "for I am hungry." But still there was no answer.

"Give me something to eat," screamed the Troll a third time: "I advise thee to do so, I say dost thou hear? otherwise I will try to wake thee."

But the girl stood stock still, whereupon he became so furious, that he gave her a kick that made the straw fly about in all directions. On seeing that, he found there was something wrong, and began to look about, and at last went down into the cellar; but both the girl's sisters

were gone, and he was now at no loss to know how all this had happened.

"Ah! thou shalt pay dearly for this," said he, taking the road to her mother's house; but when he came to the door, the gamekeeper fired, and the Troll durst not venture in, for he believed that it thundered; so he turned about to go home with all possible speed, but just as he got to the trap-door, the sun rose, and the Troll burst.*

There is plenty of gold and silver still in the mountain, if one only knew how to find the trap-door.

retold by BENJAMIN THORPE

* In a number of myths and folk-tales, the moment of the rising sun was fatal to trolls and dwarfs.

The Woman of the Sea

Shetland

One clear summer night, a young man was walking on the sand by the sea on the Isle of Unst. He had been all day in the hayfields and was come down to the shore to cool himself, for it was the full moon and the wind blowing fresh off the water.

As he came to the shore he saw the sand shining white in the moonlight and on it the sea-people dancing. He had never seen them before, for they show themselves like seals by day, but on this night, because it was midsummer and a full moon, they were dancing for joy. Here and there he saw dark patches where they had flung down their sealskins, but they themselves were as clear as the moon itself, and they cast no shadow.

He crept a little nearer, and his own shadow moved before him, and of a sudden one of the sea-people danced upon it. The dance was broken. They looked about and saw him and with a cry they fled to their sealskins and dived into the waves. The air was full of their soft crying and splashing.

But one of the fairy-people ran hither and thither on the sands, wringing her hands as if she had lost something. The young man looked and saw a patch of darkness in his own shadow. It was a seal's skin. Quickly he threw it behind a rock and watched to see what the sea-fairy would do.

She ran down to the edge of the sea and stood with her feet in the foam, crying to her people to wait for her, but they had gone too far to hear. The moon shone on her and the young man thought she was the loveliest creature he had ever seen. Then she began to weep softly to herself and the sound of it was so pitiful that he could bear it no longer. He stood upright and went down to her.

"What have you lost, woman of the sea?" he asked her.

She turned at the sound of his voice and looked at him, terrified.

For a moment he thought she was going to dive into the sea. Then she came a step nearer and held up her two hands to him.

"Sir," she said, "give it back to me and I and my people will give you the treasure of the sea." Her voice was like the waves singing in a shell.

"I would rather have you than the treasure of the sea," said the young man. Although she hid her face in her hands and fell again to crying, more hopeless than ever, he was not moved.

"It is my wife you shall be," he said. "Come with me now to the priest, and we will go home to our own house, and it is yourself shall be mistress of all I have. It is warm you will be in the long winter nights, sitting at your own hearth stone and the peat burning red, instead of swimming in the cold green sea."

She tried to tell him of the bottom of the sea where there comes neither snow nor darkness of night and the waves are as warm as a river in summer, but he would not listen. Then he threw his cloak around her and lifted her in his arms and they were married in the priest's house.

He brought her home to his little thatched cottage and into the kitchen with its earthen floor, and set her down before the hearth in the red glow of the peat. She cried out when she saw the fire, for she thought it was a strange crimson jewel.

"Have you anything as bonny as that in the sea?" he asked her, kneeling down beside her and she said, so faintly that he could scarcely hear her, "No."

"I know not what there is in the sea," he said, "but there is nothing on land as bonny as you." For the first time she ceased her crying and sat looking into the heart of the fire. It was the first thing that made her forget, even for a moment, the sea which was her home.

All the days she was in the young man's house, she never lost the wonder of the fire and it was the first thing she brought her children to see. For she had three children in the twice seven years she lived with him. She was a good wife to him. She baked his bread and she spun the wool from the fleece of his Shetland sheep.

He never named the seal's skin to her, nor she to him, and he thought she was content, for he loved her dearly and she was happy with her children. Once, when he was ploughing on the headland above the bay, he looked down and saw her standing on the rocks and crying in a mournful voice to a great seal in the water. He said nothing when he came home, for he thought to himself it was not to wonder at if she were lonely for the sight of her own people. As for the seal's skin, he had hidden it well.

There came a September evening and she was busy in the house, and the children playing hide-and-seek in the stacks in the gloaming. She heard them shouting and went out to them.

"What have you found?" she said.

The children came running to her. "It is like a big cat," they said, "but it is softer than a cat. Look!" She looked and saw her seal's skin that was hidden under last year's hay.

She gazed at it, and for a long time she stood still. It was warm dusk and the air was yellow with the afterglow of the sunset. The children had run away again, and their voices among the stacks sounded like the voices of birds. The hens were on the roost already and now and then one of them clucked in its sleep. The air was full of little friendly noises from the sleepy talking of the swallows under the thatch. The door was open and the warm smell of the baking of bread came out to her.

She turned to go in, but a small breath of wind rustled over the stacks and she stopped again. It brought a sound that she had heard so long she never seemed to hear it at all. It was the sea whispering down on the sand. Far out on the rocks the great waves broke in a boom, and close in on the sand the little waves slipped racing back. She took up the seal's skin and went swiftly down the track that led to the sands. The children saw her and cried to her to wait for them, but she did not hear them. She was just out of sight when their father came in from the byre and they ran to tell him.

"Which road did she take?" said he.

"The low road to the sea," they answered, but already their father was running to the shore. The children tried to follow him, but their voices died away behind him, so fast did he run.

As he ran across the hard sands, he saw her dive to join the big seal who was waiting for her, and he gave a loud cry to stop her. For a moment she rested on the surface of the sea, then she cried with her voice that was like the waves singing in a shell, "Fare ye well, and all good befall you, for you were a good man to me."

Then she dived to the fairy places that lie at the bottom of the sea and the big seal with her.

For a long time her husband watched for her to come back to him and the children; but she came no more.

retold by HELEN WADDELL

Johnnie in the Cradle

Scotland

A man and his wife were not long married, and they had a wee kiddie called Johnnie, but he was always crying and never satisfied. There was a neighbour near, a tailor, and it came to market day, and Johnnie was aye greeting, and never growing. And the wife wanted to get a day at the market, so the tailor said he'd stay and watch wee Johnnie. So he was sitting sewing by the fire, and a voice said: "Is ma mother and ma faither awa'?" He couldn't think it was the baby speaking, so he went and looked out of the window, but there was nothing, and he heard it again. "Is ma mother and ma faither awa'?" And there it was, sitting up, with its wee hands gripping the sides of the cradle. "There's a bottle of whisky in the press," it says. "Gie's a drink." Sure enough, there was one, and they had a drink together. Then wee Johnnie wanted a blow on the pipes, but there was not a set in the house, so he told the tailor to go and fetch a round strae* from the byre, and he played the loveliest tune on the pipes through the strae. They had a good talk together, and the wee thing said, "Is ma mother and ma faither coming home?" And when they came, there he was, "Nya, nya, nya", in the cradle. By this time the tailor knew it was a fairy they had there, so he followed the farmer into the byre, and told him all that had happened. The farmer just couldn't bring himself to believe it; so between them they hit on a contrivance. They let on that a lot of things had not been sold at the market, and there was to be a second day of it, and the tailor promised to come over again to sit by the bairn. They made a great stir about packing up, and then they went through to the barn, and listened through the

* Straw.

keek hole in the wall. "Is ma mother and ma faither gone?" said the wee thing, and the mother could just hardly believe her ears. But when they heard the piping through the cornstrae, they kent it was a fairy right enough, and the farmer went into the room, and he set the gridle on the fire and heated it red hot, and he fetched in a half bagful of horse manure, and set it on the gridle, and the wee thing looked at him with wild eyes. When he went to it to grip it, and put it on the gridle, it flew straight up the lum*, and as it went it cried out, "I wish I had been longer with my mother. I'd a kent her better."

collected by HAMISH HENDERSON

* Chimney.

Peter Bull

Denmark

There once lived in Denmark a peasant and his wife who owned a very good farm, but had no children. They often lamented to each other that they had no one of their own to inherit all the wealth that they possessed. They continued to prosper, and became rich people, but there was no heir to it all.

One year it happened that they owned a pretty little bull-calf, which they called Peter. It was the prettiest little creature they had ever seen—so beautiful and so wise that it understood everything that was said to it, and so gentle and so full of play that both the man and his wife came to be as fond of it as if it had been their own child.

One day the man said to his wife, "I wonder, now, whether our parish clerk could teach Peter to talk; in that case we could not do better than adopt him as our son, and let him inherit all that we possess."

"Well, I don't know," said his wife, "our clerk is tremendously learned, and knows much more than his Paternoster, and I could almost believe that he might be able to teach Peter to talk, for Peter has a wonderfully good head too. You might at least ask him about it."

Off went the man to the clerk, and asked him whether he thought he could teach a bull-calf that they had to speak, for they wished so much to have it as their heir.

The clerk was no fool; he looked round about to see that no one could overhear them, and said, "Oh, yes, I can easily do that, but you must not speak to anyone about it. It must be done in all secrecy, and the priest must not know of it, otherwise I shall get into trouble, as it is forbidden. It will also cost you something, as some very expensive books are required."

That did not matter at all, the man said; they would not care so very much what it cost. The clerk could have a hundred dollars to begin with to buy the books. He also promised to tell no one about it, and to bring the calf round in the evening.

He gave the clerk the hundred dollars on the spot, and in the evening took the calf round to him, and the clerk promised to do his best with it. In a week's time he came back to the clerk to hear about the calf and see how it was thriving. The clerk, however, said that he could not get a sight of it, for then Peter would long after him and forget all that he had already learned. He was getting on well with his learning, but another hundred dollars were needed, as they must have more books. The peasant had the money with him, so he gave it to the clerk, and went home again with high hopes.

In another week the man came again to learn what progress Peter had made now.

"He is getting on very well," said the clerk.

"I suppose he can't say anything yet?" said the man.

"Oh, yes," said the clerk, "he can say 'Moo' now."

"Do you think he will get on with his learning?" asked the peasant.

"Oh, yes," said the clerk, "but I shall want another hundred dollars for books. Peter can't learn well out of the ones that he has got."

"Well, well," said the man, "what must be spent *shall* be spent."

So he gave the clerk the third hundred dollars for books, and a cask of good old ale for Peter. The clerk drank the ale himself, and gave the calf milk, which he thought would be better for it.

Some weeks passed, during which the peasant did not come round to ask after the calf, being frightened lest it should cost him another hundred dollars, for he had begun to squirm a bit at having to part with so much money. Meanwhile the clerk decided that the calf was as fat as it could be, so he killed it. After he had got all the beef out of the way he went inside, put on his black clothes, and made his way to the peasant's house.

As soon as he had said "Good-day" he asked, "Has Peter come home here?"

"No, indeed, he hasn't," said the man; "surely he hasn't run away?"

"I hope," said the clerk, "that he would not behave so contempt-ibly after all the trouble I have had to teach him, and all that I have spent upon him. I have had to spend at least a hundred dollars of my own money to buy books for him before I got him so far on. He could say anything he liked now, so he said to-day that he longed to see his parents again. I was willing to give him that pleasure, but I was afraid that he wouldn't be able to find the way here by himself, so I made myself ready to go with him. When he had got outside the house I remembered that I had left my stick inside, and went in again to get it. When I came out again Peter had gone off on his own account. I thought he would be here, and if he isn't I don't know where he is."

The peasant and his wife began to lament bitterly that Peter had run away in this fashion just when they were to have so much joy of him, and after they had spent so much on his education. The worst of it was that now they had no heir after all. The clerk comforted them as best he could; he also was greatly distressed that Peter should have behaved in such a way just when he should have gained honour from his pupil. Perhaps he had only gone astray, and he would advertise him at church next Sunday, and find out whether anyone had seen him. Then he bade them "Good-bye," and went home and dined on a good fat veal roast.

Now it so happened that the clerk took in a newspaper, and one day he chanced to read in its columns of a new merchant who had settled in a town at some distance, and whose name was "Peter Bull". He put the newspaper in his pocket, and went round to the sorrowing couple who had lost their heir. He read the paragraph to them, and added, "I wonder, now, whether that could be your bull-calf Peter?"

"Yes, of course it is," said the man; "who else would it be?"

His wife then spoke up and said, "You must set out, good man, and see about him, for it *is* him, I am perfectly certain. Take a good sum of money with you, too; for who knows but what he may want some cash now that he has turned a merchant!"

Next day the man got a bag of money on his back and a sandwich in his pocket, and his pipe in his mouth, and set out for the town where the new merchant lived. It was no short way, and he travelled for many days before he finally arrived there. He reached it one morning, just at daybreak, found out the right place, and asked if the merchant was at home. Yes, he was, said the people, but he was not up yet.

"That doesn't matter," said the peasant, "for I am his father. Just show me up to his bedroom."

He was shown up to the room, and as soon as he entered it, and caught sight of the merchant, he recognized him at once. He had the same broad forehead, the same thick neck, and same red hair, but in other respects he was now like a human being. The peasant rushed straight up to him and took a firm hold of him. "O Peter," said he, "what a sorrow you have caused us, both myself and your mother, by running off like this just as we had got you well educated! Get up, now, so that I can see you properly, and have a talk with you."

The merchant thought that it was a lunatic who had made his way in to him, and thought it best to take things quietly.

"All right," said he, "I shall do so at once." He got out of bed and made haste to dress himself.

"Ay," said the peasant, "now I can see how clever our clerk is. He has done well by you, for now you look just like a human being. If one didn't know it, one would never think that it was you we got from the red cow; will you come home with me now?"

"No," said the merchant, "I can't find time just now. I have a big business to look after."

"You could have the farm at once, you know," said the peasant, "and we old people would retire. But if you would rather stay in business, of course you may do so. Are you in want of anything?"

"Oh, yes," said the merchant; "I want nothing so much as money. A merchant has always a use for that."

"I can well believe that," said the peasant, "for you had nothing at all to start with. I have brought some with me for that very end." With that he emptied his bag of money out upon the table, so that it was all covered with bright dollars.

When the merchant saw what kind of man he had before him he began to speak him fair, and invited him to stay with him for some days, so that they might have some more talk together.

"Very well," said the peasant, "but you must call me 'Father'."

"I have neither father nor mother alive," said Peter Bull.

"I know that," said the man; "your real father was sold at Hamburg last Michaelmas, and your real mother died while calving in spring; but my wife and I have adopted you as our own, and you are our only heir, so you must call me 'Father'."

Peter Bull was quite willing to do so, and it was settled that he should keep the money, while the peasant made his will and left to him all that he had, before he went home to his wife, and told her the whole story.

She was delighted to hear that it was true enough about Peter Bull—that he was no other than their own bull-calf.

"You must go at once and tell the clerk," said she, "and pay him the hundred dollars of his own money that he spent upon our son. He has earned them well, and more besides, for all the joy he has given us in having such a son and heir."

The man agreed with this, and thanked the clerk for all he had done, and gave him two hundred dollars. Then he sold the farm, and removed with his wife to the town where their dear son and heir was living. To him they gave all their wealth, and lived with him till their dying day.

retold by ANDREW LANG

The Juniper Tree

Germany

A long while ago, at least two thousand years, there lived a rich man who had a good and beautiful wife. They loved one another very dearly; but they had no children; and she prayed and longed for a child with a great longing.

Now in the courtyard that lay beneath the windows of the house in which they lived there stood a juniper tree which, however long the night or sharp the frost, was never without its dark-green, needle-pointed leaves. And one sunlit winter's day as she was standing beneath it, paring an apple, she cut her finger, and the drops of blood trickled down from her finger on to the snow.

"Ah!" said she, with a sigh as she gazed at it, "how happy should I be if only I had a child, as white as that snow, as red as that blood!"

As she uttered these words, her heart lightened, a wild joy sprang up in her, and she knew that her wish would come true. The happy days went by. When winter was gone and its snows had melted away, the meadows began to grow green again. April came; the woods and fields were sweet with the flowers of spring; the trees put forth their green leaves; the wild cherries shed their petals upon the ground; and the birds poured out their songs, daybreak to evening, in the woods and groves. Then followed summer. The small spicy flowers of the juniper began to unfold, her heart leapt within her at their fragrance, and she fell on her knees, beside herself for joy. When autumn drew near, ripening fruit hung thick upon the trees; and one still and lovely evening she ate greedily of the juniper berries. But after that she began to be sick and sad and sorrowful. And when the eighth month was passed, she called her husband to her, wept, and said, "If I should die, then I pray thee bury me under this juniper tree."

Not long after this, her child was born—the child of her desire, and lovely; as red as blood, as white as snow; but she herself was weak and wearied out. As soon as she had looked upon it, an exceeding great joy overcame her, and she fainted away and died.

Her husband buried her under the juniper tree, and wept and mourned over her. But in time his grief began to abate, and he to forget. And at length he dried his tears, and took to himself another wife.

Time passed on, and a daughter was born to her; but the child of his first wife was a boy. The mother loved and doted on her daughter, but she hated her stepson. She knew that he would inherit her husband's possessions, and the very sight and thought of him cut her to the heart. And she began to think how she might get everything for her daughter only. So she treated him very harshly, half starved him, never let him rest, and would beat and punish him for no fault and without reason, so that he went continually in fear of her and could find no place in the house to play in, or be at peace. And as time went by her cruelty increased, and she hated him more and more.

Now it happened one day, when the mother was in her store-room, that her little girl ran up to her, and said, "Mother, may I have an apple?"

"Why, yes, my pretty dear," she said; and gave her a ripe rosy apple out of her apple-chest. Now this chest had a heavy and cumbersome lid, and was fitted with a broad sharp lock of iron.

"Mother," said the little girl, "may I have an apple for my little brother too?"

A pang of envy and jealousy went through the woman's breast, but she showed no sign of it. "Yes, indeed, my child," she said. "When he comes in from school, he too shall have an apple."

As she was speaking, she happened to look out of the window and saw the little boy in the distance coming home from school. At sight of him the Evil One entered into her heart. She took back the apple she had given her daughter, threw it into the apple-chest and shut down the lid, telling her that she should have an even sweeter one before she went to bed.

When the little boy came in at the door, she was lying in wait for him, and alone; and she said to him in a small wheedling voice, her face cold and grey with wickedness, "Come in, my dear, and I will give you an apple."

The little boy gazed at her. "Thank you, Mother," he said. "I should like to have an apple. But how strange and dreadful you look!"

It seemed to her that she was compelled to listen to a voice within her. "Look!" she said. "Come with me." And she took him in secret into her store-room, lifted the heavy lid of the chest, and said, "There, you shall choose one for yourself."

So he came near, and as he stooped himself over the edge of the apple-chest to do as she had bidden him, of a sudden and with all her force she let fall the lid with its iron lock upon his neck, and his head fell off among the apples.

When she lifted the lid and saw what she had done, she was stricken with terror, not knowing—when her husband came home—how she should explain this dreadful thing and free herself from it. She sat down to think. And presently she stole upstairs into an upper room, took a white linen handkerchief out of a drawer, and having returned to the chest, set the little boy's head upon his narrow shoulders again, tied the handkerchief round his neck, and carrying him out, seated him on a stool in the yard and put an apple in his hand.

Not long after this her little daughter came running into the kitchen to her mother, who was standing bent double by the fire, stirring the soup in a great caldron that had been prepared for her husband's supper.

"Mother," said she, "little brother is sitting in the garden with an apple in his hand. I asked him to give me a taste, but he didn't answer me. And his face looked so pale and still that I was frightened."

"Nonsense, child!" said her mother. "Go back to him. Speak to him again, and if he refuses to answer you, give him a sound box on the ear. That will call him to his senses."

The child went back, and said, "Brother, please, please give me a taste of your apple." But the mouth answered never a word; so she hit him lightly on the cheek; and immediately his head fell off. At sight of it she was terrified and ran screaming back to her mother, and hid her eyes in her lap. She wept and wept and would not be comforted.

"My dear, my own pretty dear!" cried her mother; "what have you done! Alas, what dreadful thing is this! But hold your tongue. Let nobody hear of it. Leave all to me." And she took the body of the little boy, cut it into pieces, and put them into the caldron.

When her husband came home and sat down to supper, he asked her, "Where is my son?"

She made no answer, as if she had not heard; and served up a great bowl of black soup upon the table. And the girl sat silently weeping.

"I asked," said the man again, "where is my son?"

"Your son?" said the woman. "A friend of his mother's came and has taken him away to stay with his great-uncle."

"Taken him away!" said her husband. "But he did not even stay to bid goodbye to me."

"He begged me to let him go," said the woman. "He cried to go. Again and again I said, 'No; your father will miss you.' He would not listen. He is a stubborn child. But, why trouble? He will be well taken care of."

"Ay," said her husband; "but I am grieved to think of it. He should not have gone away without wishing me goodbye." He turned away from her. "Weep no more, child," he said to his daughter. "Your brother will come back again."

With that he began to eat. But he stayed sad and sorrowful, and as he ate, his misery increased with his hunger and it seemed he could never be satisfied. His supper done, he went out alone, his mind tormented with dread and horror. And his wife took the great caldron and in the dusk of the evening emptied out what was in it on the stones of the yard—soup, bones and all.

But her little daughter had been watching all that she did; and on seeing this, went softly upstairs and fetched a brightly coloured silk handkerchief, which her father had given her, from out of a drawer. With this she crept downstairs again and out into the garden. There she wrapped up the bones in her handkerchief, as if in a shroud, and, weeping bitterly, carried them out into the yard and laid them under the juniper tree.

And in the quiet of the evening the juniper tree began to bestir itself, and its branches to sway gently to and fro, to open out their bushy-green leaves, and as gently bring them together again, like a child softly clapping its hands for gladness. At the same time a little cloud, as it were, seemed to arise from out of the midst of the tree, and within the cloud there burned a radiance as of a fire. And there fluttered up from out of the fire a bird marvellous in beauty, which mounted into the air and, singing wildly and sweetly, flew away. When the bird had vanished into the evening, the branches of the juniper tree became still and dark again; and the bones that had lain at the foot of the tree were there no longer. At this the little girl was comforted, and her heart leapt for joy. It was as if she knew that her brother who had been dead was now alive again. She went merrily into the house, sat down to her supper, and ate.

The night went by; and early the next morning the bird that had soared up from out of the tree came flying over the village and

alighted on the roof of the house of a goldsmith. And there it began to warble and sing.

> *"My mother slew her little son;*
> *My father thought me lost and gone:*
> *Out in the dusk on the darkening stones*
> *She flung in hatred my poor bones.*
> *My gentle sister pitied me,*
> *And laid me under the juniper tree;*
> *Now, now I wander merrily,*
> *Over hill and dale I fly.*
> Soo-eet, soo-eet—
> Ki-weet, ki-weet:
> *Oh, what a happy bird am I!"*

Now the goldsmith in his apron was sitting in his workshop fitting together the last links of a slender gold chain. When he heard the strange bird singing on the housetop he rose from his stool so suddenly that one of his slippers fell off. Without staying to put it on again, his chain in one hand, his pincers in the other, he ran out into the street and gazed up at the bird, its bright feathers burnished with the shining of the sun. And he said to the bird, "A marvellous sweet song that was, my pretty bird. Pray sing it to me again and I shall hear every single note of it."

"Nay," answered the bird. "I may not sing twice for nothing. But give me that chain of gold, and I will sing again gladly."

It swooped down from the roof, and perching on the goldsmith's shoulder sang its song again, took the slender chain of gold in its claw, and flew away, until it came to the house of a cobbler who was sitting within mending a shoe.

At sound of its first few notes, the cobbler was spellbound; he called his wife and his children, boys and girls, to come and listen; and there they all stood in the sunny street, their eyes fixed on this strange bird, that had now fallen silent. "A marvellous sweet song, that was," he said. "Pray, pretty bird, sing it all over again."

"Nay," answered the bird; "I may not sing twice for nothing."

At this the cobbler bade his wife run upstairs to the garret. "On the topmost shelf of the cupboard," he told her, "you will find a pair of small red shoes of the finest leather ever made. Bring them down to me."

At sight of the shoes, the bird came near, took them dangling in its other claw, returned to the gable of the cobbler's house, and repeated its song.

And when the song was over, with the golden chain in its one claw, the red shoes in the other, it flew away, far away, until it came to a mill, where on a green bank beside the mill-dam sat a miller with his men hicking and hacking at a new mill-stone. *Hick-hack, hick-hack* went their mallets and chisels: *Klippity-klop, klippity-klop* went the old mill-wheel. And the bird, having perched on the branch of a linden tree that stood near at hand, began to sing.

>   *"My mother slew her little son . . ."*

The miller stopped working to listen:

>   *"My father thought me lost and gone . . ."*

One of his men began listening:

>   *"Out in the dusk on the darkening stones*
>   *She flung in hatred my poor bones . . ."*

And another:

>   *"My gentle sister pitied me,*
>   *And laid me under the juniper tree . . ."*

And yet another:

>   *"Now, now I wander merrily,*
>   *Over hill and dale I fly.*
>   *Soo-eet, soo-eet—*
>   *Ki-weet, ki-weet:*
>   *Oh, what a happy bird am I!"*

Now all had stopped working and were listening. And the miller—beside himself with delight at the song and at the bird itself, with its sunlit shimmering feathers, red and emerald, the bright golden ring about its neck, and eyes which glittered like dark clear waterdrops as it gazed down on them—besought it with tears in his own to sing again.

"Nay," answered the bird; "I may not sing twice for nothing. Give me that nether mill-stone and I will most gladly."

To the amazement of the miller, the bird flew down among them, and when he and his men had heaved up the heavy mill-stone upon its edge, it thrust its gentle head through the hole which they had pierced in the middle of the stone, and flew back again into the linden tree. There it repeated its song.

When its last note had died away and the dull *klippity-klop,
klippity-klop* of the mill-wheel was heard again, it spread its wings,
and—the mill-stone about its neck, the chain of gold in one claw, the
red shoes in the other—it flew and flew until it came and
alighted on the roof of the house in the courtyard of which stood the
juniper tree from whence it had sprung. There it stayed silent a
while.

And the three of them—the man and his wife and the little
girl—were sitting within the house at meat.

"I know not why," said the father; "but I feel lighter in spirit than
for many hours past. It may be because the sun is shining; it may be a
friend is coming, bringing good news."

At this moment, the bird flew down from the roof of the house
and perched above its porch.

"Good news, forsooth!" cried the woman. "Or *evil*. You must be
mad, husband. There is thunder in the air; it's growing dark. I am in
a fever; my teeth keep chattering; my heart is like lead in my body."

She tore open her bodice with a shuddering sigh.

But the little girl sat listening, the tears from her eyes dropping
slowly down upon her plate, half for joy and half for sadness; for the
bird above the porch had begun to sing—although the words of its
song came but faintly to the ears of those who were sitting within the
house.

At its close, the man rose from his chair. "Never in all the days of
my life," he said, "have I heard bird sing a song so strange and so
marvellous sweet as that. I must go out and see. It may be, if we do
not scare it away, it can be enticed to sing again."

"Go out! No!" said the woman. "I entreat you not to leave me.
There is dread and danger in the air. The blood in my veins runs like
fire. I am sick, and must die."

But he was gone, and the bird had begun to sing again:

> *"My mother slew her little son;
> My father thought me lost and gone . . ."*

With these words, the bird so let fall the golden chain dangling from
its claw that it encircled his neck. Filled with delight, he hastened
back into the house.

"See," he said, "what this magical and marvellous bird has given
me, a necklet of the finest gold!"

At this, the little girl also got up from her stool and ran out. And
the bird had been singing on:

"Out in the dusk on the darkening stones
She flung in hatred my poor bones.
My gentle sister pitied me,
And laid me under the juniper tree...."

At this, the bird let fall the bright red-leather shoes at her feet. She ran back, wild with joy.

"Look, look, dear father," she cried; "see what the bird has brought for me!"

"Now, now I wander merrily,
Over hill and dale I fly.
Soo-eet, soo-eet—
Ki-weet, ki-weet:
Oh, what a happy bird am I!"

The song had come to an end, and again there was silence both in the house and out. At this, the woman could endure herself no longer. Her face was grey and drawn with misery.

"I cannot breathe," she said. "It is as though the world were coming to an end. O, where to hide myself! I must be gone."

But as she stepped beyond the threshold of the house and out from the porch, the bird let fall the mill-stone upon her, and without sigh or sound, she fell dead in the shadow of the juniper tree.

At noise of her fall, the father and the little girl ran out of the house; and lo, there, under the juniper tree, stood the little boy, come back from his enchantment. He leapt into his father's arms. They wept together for joy, the man and his two children, and returned into the house.

collected by JACOB and WILHELM GRIMM
retold by Walter de la Mare

ᏸᏸᏸ

The Rich Farmer and the Poor Farmer
Iceland

ᏸᏸᏸ

Two farmers once lived in the same parish. They happened to have the same name, but in all other respects they were as different from one another as might be, both in circumstances and in character. One was so rich that he could scarcely count his own wealth, while the other was so poor that he hardly knew where the next meal was coming from, either for his folk or for himself.

Times were hard in the neighbourhood where the two namesakes lived. There were many poor, and it was the habit of the rich farmer to house a number of these unfortunates. Never were they so many that he turned one away from his door. However, some of his neighbours thought it strange that these poor people appeared to vanish, and no one ever discovered what became of them. The rumour began to get around that he murdered the poor wretches to be rid of them. Nothing came of it, though, except that his neighbours took to avoiding his house and never went there unless compelled by urgent business. Only his namesake, the poor farmer, refused to believe the rumour. Nevertheless he felt that there was something strange about his friend's behaviour.

So the days passed by. Then one morning the poor farmer awoke in his bed with a fearful start and a fit of sobbing. His wife was troubled by this, and asked him what the matter was. He replied that he had dreamed of a man who had come to him. He had been of noble appearance and all shining, and he had told him that after three days he and his rich namesake would both die, and their souls would keep company beyond the grave. This news he was to pass on to his neighbour. Beside the sorrow of parting from his wife and children, he said, what oppressed his mind was the thought of having to share his neighbour's company in the next world, and the uncertainty whither this might lead him. However, there was nothing for it but to do as he had been bidden and pass on the news.

The poor farmer now got ready, and saying goodbye to his wife and children, he set off for his neighbour's house.

The rich farmer was standing outside when he arrived. He greeted him cheerfully and asked whether he had any news to tell. His poor namesake replied gloomily that there was not much worth telling. The other now tried to find out the cause of his melancholy, and learned of the dream. He said that he saw no reason for sadness in this, for all men had to die sooner or later. He asked his namesake into the parlour and had food put before him, and was himself as cheerful as could be; but the poor farmer was able to eat nothing for worry.

The rich farmer said that they would do best to stay together for the few days of life that remained to them. With so little time left there was a great deal to be done; for they must attend to the disposal of their goods. The poor farmer became gloomier than ever when he heard this, thinking that they would do much better to prepare for death in a different way. He said as much to his friend, but he replied that there was no time for such thoughts as yet. And so it was, as he would have it: they spent all that day going round the farm and to all the folk of his household, while he gave orders and disposed of his possessions down to the last detail, as though this was the most natural thing in the world.

That night the two neighbours shared the same bed. The next morning the rich farmer was up early and in a gay mood. He said that they could not afford to give themselves a holiday yet, for there was still much to do. Now they must take a trip to the village, for he had to go over his account at the store. His namesake wanted nothing so much as to stay quietly at home and prepare himself for death, but again the other had his way. They rode to the village and the rich farmer was all day going over his account, while his friend had nothing to do but suffer agonies of anxiety for his heedlessness and levity. It seemed quite clear that he had no thought for anything but his wealth and worldly pleasures. Nevertheless at the last he ordered large sums from his trading credit to be transferred to the accounts of various needy folk. The poor farmer noticed this, and it now occurred to him that perhaps his namesake was not so utterly without better feelings after all.

That night they returned home and slept as before. On the morning of the third day the rich farmer was afoot earlier than ever, saying that there was still much to be done and they must make the most of their last day. As before, the other pleaded for peace; but to no avail. As ever, his neighbour had his way. Horses were brought saddled to the door, and they mounted and rode off.

They now took a narrow pathway that led over hill and dale to a little valley, where green meadows lay between wooded slopes. Here they came upon a fine-looking farmstead, and many folk, both young and old, appeared to welcome the rich farmer, calling him father. His poor companion now recognized in them those homeless and destitute ones who had formerly been housed by his neighbour.

They spent most of the day in this place, the rich farmer talking with his people, giving them advice, and making all needful arrangements. Finally, when they took their leave, everyone followed them on their way, bidding the rich farmer farewell with tears of regret.

On the way back, the rich farmer asked his namesake whether he would not first go to his own home and say goodbye to his wife and children, for he would not see them again. To this the other gladly agreed, and was now of quite a different mind about his friend than he had been before. The two stayed for a while at this dwelling, and the rich farmer comforted his friend's wife, giving her much good advice, and on parting he made over a generous portion of land to her.

As they continued on their way, the rich farmer asked his friend what opinion he had of his present company and future prospects. The other was almost in tears at this, and answered that things were very different from what had been rumoured, and he could see nothing but good. What had men thought about his poor people? asked the other, and he was told that rumours had made him guilty of their destruction. The rich farmer then said that of course there had really been no need for him to ask, for it had not escaped his notice how all had avoided him and his house, with the exception of his friend. The latter declared that he was glad he had not judged him so harshly as the rest, for he now saw clearly that the rumours had been quite groundless.

That night, as before, the two went to bed together. But next morning, when somebody came to call them, they were both dead.

In accordance with the rich farmer's will, they were both buried in the same grave.

collected by JÓN ÁRNASON and MAGNÚS GRÍMSSON
translated by Alan Boucher

Toller's Neighbours

Denmark

Once upon a time a young man and a young girl were in service together at a mansion down near Klode Mill, in the district of Lysgaard. They became attached to each other, and as they both were honest and faithful servants, their master and mistress had a great regard for them, and gave them a wedding dinner the day they were married. Their master gave them also a little cottage with a little field, and there they went to live.

This cottage lay in the middle of a wild heath, and the surrounding country was in bad repute; for in the neighbourhood were a number of old grave-mounds, which it was said were inhabited by the Mount-folk; though Toller, so the peasant was called, cared little for that. "When one only trusts in God," thought Toller, "and does what is just and right to all men, one need not be afraid of anything." They had now taken possession of their cottage and moved in all their little property. When the man and his wife, late one evening, were sitting talking together as to how they could best manage to get on in the world, they heard a knock at the door, and on Toller opening it, in walked a little little man, and wished them "Good evening." He had a red cap on his head, a long beard and long hair, a large hump on his back, and a leathern apron before him, in which was stuck a hammer. They immediately knew him to be a Troll; notwithstanding he looked so good-natured and friendly, that they were not at all afraid of him.

"Now hear, Toller," said the little stranger, "I see well enough that you know who I am, and matters stand thus: I am a poor little hill-man, to whom people have left no other habitation on earth than the graves of fallen warriors, or mounds, where the rays of the sun never can shine down upon us. We have heard that you are come to live here, and our king is fearful that you will do us harm, and even destroy us. He has, therefore, sent me up to you this evening, that I should beg of you, as amicably as I could, to allow us to hold our dwellings in peace. You shall never be annoyed by us, or disturbed by us in your pursuits."

"Be quite at your ease, good man," said Toller, "I have never injured any of God's creatures willingly, and the world is large enough for us all, I believe; and I think we can manage to agree, without the one having any need to do mischief to the other."

"Well, thank God!" exclaimed the little man, beginning in his joy to dance about the room, "that is excellent, and we will in return do you all the good in our power, and that you will soon discover; but now I must depart."

"Will you not first take a spoonful of supper with us?" asked the wife, setting a dish of porridge down on the stool near the window; for the Man of the Mount was so little that he could not reach up to the table. "No, I thank you," said the mannikin, "our king is impatient for my return, and it would be a pity to let him wait for the good news I have to tell him." Hereupon the little man bade them farewell and went his way.

From that day forwards, Toller lived in peace and concord with the little people of the Mount. They could see them go in and out of their mounds in daylight, and no one ever did anything to vex them. At length they became so familiar, that they went in and out of Toller's house, just as if it had been their own. Sometimes it happened that they would borrow a pot or a copper-kettle from the kitchen, but always brought it back again, and set it carefully on the same spot from which they had taken it. They also did all the service they could in return. When the spring came, they would come out of their mounds in the night, gather all the stones off the arable land, and lay them in a heap along the furrows. At harvest time they would pick up all the ears of corn, that nothing might be lost to Toller. All this was observed by the farmer, who, when in bed, or when he read his evening prayer, often thanked the Almighty for having given him the Mount-folk for neighbours. At Easter and Whitsuntide, or in the Christmas holidays, he always set a dish of nice milk-porridge for them, as good as it could be made, out on the mound.

Once, after having given birth to a daughter, his wife was so ill that Toller thought she was near her end. He consulted all the cunning people in the district, but no one knew what to prescribe for her recovery. He sat up every night and watched over the sufferer, that he might be at hand to administer to her wants. Once he fell asleep, and on opening his eyes again towards morning, he saw the room full of the Mount-folk: one sat and rocked the baby, another was busy in cleaning the room, a third stood by the pillow of the sick woman and made a drink of some herbs, which he gave his wife. As soon as they observed that Toller was awake they all ran out of the room; but from that night the poor woman began to mend, and before a fortnight was past she was able to leave her bed and go about her household work, well and cheerful as before.

Another time, Toller was in trouble for want of money to get his horses shod before he went to the town. He talked the matter over with his wife, and they knew not well what course to adopt. But when they were in bed his wife said: "Art thou asleep, Toller?" "No," he answered, "what is it?" "I think," said she, "there is something the matter with the horses in the stable, they are making such a disturbance." Toller rose, lighted his lantern, and went to the stable, and, on opening the door, found it full of the little Mount-folk. They had made the horses lie down, because the mannikins could not reach up to them. Some were employed in taking off the old shoes, some were filing the heads of the nails, while others were tacking on the new shoes; and the next morning, when Toller took his horses to water, he found them shod so beautifully that the best of smiths could not have shod them better. In this manner the Mount-folk and Toller rendered all the good services they could to each other, and many years passed pleasantly. Toller began to grow an old man, his daughter was grown up, and his circumstances were better every year. Instead of the little cottage in which he began the world, he now owned a large and handsome house, and the naked wild heath was converted into fruitful arable land.

One evening just before bed-time, someone knocked at the door, and the Man of the Mount walked in. Toller and his wife looked at him with surprise; for the mannikin was not in his usual dress. He wore on his head a shaggy cap, a woollen kerchief round his throat, and a great sheep-skin cloak covered his body. In his hand he had a stick, and his countenance was very sorrowful. He brought a greeting to Toller from the king, who requested that he, his wife, and little Inger would come over to them in the Mount that evening, for the king had a matter of importance, about which he wished to talk with him. The tears ran down the little man's cheeks while he said this, and when Toller tried to comfort him, and inquired into the source of his trouble, the Man of the Mount only wept the more, but would not impart the cause of his grief.

Toller, his wife and daughter, then went over to the Mount. On descending into the cave, they found it decorated with bunches of sweet willow, crowsfoot, and other flowers, that were to be found on the heath. A large table was spread from one end of the cave to the other. When the peasant and his family entered, they were placed at the head of the table by the side of the king. The little folk also took their places, and began to eat, but they were far from being as cheerful as usual; they sat and sighed and hung down their heads; and it was easy to see that something had gone amiss with them. When the repast was finished, the king said to Toller: "I invited you to come over to us because we all wished to thank you for having been so kind and friendly to us, during the whole time we have been neighbours. But now there are so many churches built in the land, and all of them have such great bells, which ring so loud morning and evening, that we can bear it no longer; we are, therefore, going to leave Jutland and pass over to Norway, as the great number of our people have done long ago. We now wish you farewell, Toller, as we must part."

When the king had said this, all the Mount-folk came and took Toller by the hand, and bade him farewell, and the same to his wife. When they came to Inger, they said: "To you, dear Inger, we will give a remembrance of us, that you may think of the little Mount-people when they are far away." And as they said this, each took up a stone from the ground and threw it into Inger's apron. They left the Mount one by one, with the king leading the way.

Toller and his family remained standing on the Mount as long as they could discern them. They saw the little Trolls wandering over the heath, each with a wallet on his back and a stick in his hand. When they had gone a good part of the way, to where the road leads down to the sea, they all turned round once more, and waved their hands, to say farewell. Then they disappeared, and Toller saw them no more. Sorrowfully he returned to his home.

The next morning Inger saw that all the small stones the Mount-folk had thrown into her apron shone and sparkled, and were real precious stones. Some were blue, others brown, white, and black, and it was the Trolls who had imparted the colour of their eyes to the stones, that Inger might remember them when they were gone; and all the precious stones which we now see, shine and sparkle only because the Mount-folk have given them the colour of their eyes, and it was some of these beautiful precious stones which they once gave to Inger.

retold by BENJAMIN THORPE

Door Prayer at Evening

Iceland

Guard the door, good Lord, this night,
Gracious, by thy Cross its might:
Windows, walls, roofs, floors and houses,
As thy darkness round us closes,
Here the Holy Ghost do dwell,
Fend us from the Fiend of Hell,
And all his imps be barred as well.

God keep the door and Crux the lock, Mary Maiden all within and Michael Angel all without; may none break down the goodman's door.

Out Gurg,
In Jesus.
Out Gassagull,
In God's angel,
Out Regarist,
In Jesus Christ.
Out Maledictus,
In Benedictus.

Into God's keeping we commend us all, and good night.

collected by JÓN ÁRNASON and MAGNÚS GRÍMSSON
translated by Alan Boucher

Bibliography

1. Collectors, authors, translators and books represented in this anthology and other recommended books

ASBJÖRNSEN, PETER C. and MOE, JORGEN I. *Popular Tales from the Norse*. Edmonston and Douglas, Edinburgh, 1859. Reissued by The Bodley Head, London, 1969.

BARRETT, W. H. *Tales from the Fens*. Edited by Enid Porter. Routledge and Kegan Paul, London, 1963.
More Tales from the Fens. Edited by Enid Porter. Routledge and Kegan Paul, London, 1964.

BOSSCHÈRE, JEAN DE and MORRIS, M. C. O. *Christmas Tales of Flanders*. Heinemann, London, 1917. Reissued by Dover Publications, New York, 1972.

BOUCHER, ALAN. *Ghosts, Witchcraft and the Other World* (Icelandic folktales I) Iceland Review Library, Reykjavik, 1977. These are translations of material collected by Jón Árnason and Magnús Grímsson. The second and third volumes, also translated by Alan Boucher, are *Elves, Trolls and Elemental Beings* and *Adventures, Outlaws and Past Events*.

BRIGGS, KATHARINE M. *A Dictionary of British Folk-Tales*. Four volumes. Routledge and Kegan Paul, London, 1970–1.

BRIGGS, KATHARINE and TONGUE, RUTH L. *Folktales of England*. (*Folktales of the World* series.) Routledge and Kegan Paul, London, 1965.

CHAMBERS, ROBERT. *Popular Rhymes, Fireside Stories, and Amusements, of Scotland*. William and Robert Chambers, Edinburgh, 1842.

COLWELL, EILEEN. *Round About and Long Ago*. Tales from the English Counties. Longman Young Books, London, 1972.
Tales from the Islands. Kestrel, London, 1975.

CRAIGIE, WILLIAM A. *Scandinavian Folklore*. Gardner, Paisley and London, 1896.

CUTT, NANCY and W. TOWRIE. *The Hogboon of Hell and other Strange Orkney Tales*. André Deutsch, London, 1979.

DENNISON, WALTER TRAILL. *Orkney Folklore and Traditions*. Edited by Ernest W. Marwick. Herald Press, Kirkwall, 1961.

GRIMM, JACOB L. K. and WILHELM. *About Wise Men and Simpletons*. Translated by Elizabeth Shub. Hamish Hamilton, London, 1972.
The Complete Grimm's Fairy Tales. Routledge and Kegan Paul, London, 1975. This collection by an unnamed translator was first published by Pantheon Books Inc., New York, in 1944.
Grimm's Fairy Tales. Penguin Books, Harmondsworth, 1948. Reissued 1971.
Grimm's Tales for Old and Young. Translated by Ralph Manheim. Victor Gollancz, London, 1978.
Popular Folk Tales. Translated by Brian Alderson. Victor Gollancz, London, 1978.

GRUNDTVIG, SVENDT. *Danish Fairy Tales*. Translated by J. Grant Cramer. Four Seas Company. 1919. Reissued by Dover Publications, New York, 1972.

HALLIWELL, JAMES ORCHARD. *Popular Rhymes and Nursery Tales of England*. John Russell Smith, London, 1849. Reissued by The Bodley Head, London, 1970.

HARTLAND, EDWIN SIDNEY. *English Fairy and other Folk Tales*. The Camelot Classics, London, 1886.

HAUFF, WILHELM. *Fairy Tales of Wilhelm Hauff*. Translated by Anthea Bell. Abelard Schuman, London, 1969.

JACOBS, JOSEPH. *English Fairy Tales*. David Nutt, London, 1890.
More English Fairy Tales. David Nutt, London, 1894.
These two volumes were combined and reissued under the title *English Fairy Tales* by The Bodley Head, London, 1968.

JONES, GWYN. *Scandinavian Legends and Folk-Tales*. Oxford University Press, London, 1956.

KEIGHTLEY, THOMAS. *The Fairy Mythology*. Two volumes. William Harrison Ainsworth, London, 1828. Revised and enlarged edition, H. G. Bohn, London, 1850.

LANG, ANDREW. *The Fairy Tale Books of Many Colours*. This twelve-volume series of translations and retellings of the folk-tales of the world was published by Longmans, Green in London between 1888 and 1910 and reissued by Dover Publications, New York, between 1965 and 1968.

OPIE, IONA and PETER. *The Classic Fairy Tales*. Oxford University Press, London, 1974.

PICARD, BARBARA LEONIE. *German Hero-Tales and Folk Sagas*. Oxford University Press, London, 1959.

REEVES, JAMES. *English Fables and Fairy Stories*. Oxford University Press, London, 1954.

SIMPSON, JACQUELINE. *Icelandic Folktales and Legends*. B. T. Batsford, London, 1972. This book consists of translations of folk material collected by Jón Árnason.

Legends of Icelandic Magicians. Boydell and Brewer (for The Folklore Society), Cambridge, 1975. Translations from Jón Árnason, Ólafur Davídsson and directly from oral tradition.

STARKEY, DINAH. *Ghosts and Bogles*. Good Reading, London, 1977.

THORPE, BENJAMIN. *Northern Mythology*. Three volumes. Edward Lumley, London, 1851.

Yule-Tide Stories: A Collection of Scandinavian and North-German Popular Tales and Traditions. Henry G. Bohn, London, 1853.

WADDELL, HELEN. *The Princess Splendour and Other Stories*. Longman, London, 1969.

WILLIAMS-ELLIS, A. *British Fairy Tales*. Blackie, London, 1976.

WILSON, BARBARA KER. *Scottish Folk-Tales and Legends*. Oxford University Press, London, 1954.

2. Reference Books

BETTELHEIM, BRUNO. *The Uses of Enchantment—The Meaning and Importance of Fairy Tales*. Knopf, New York, 1976; Penguin Books, Harmondsworth, 1978.

COOK, ELIZABETH. *The Ordinary and the Fabulous: An Introduction to Myths, Legends and Fairy Tales*. Cambridge University Press, London, 1969. Second edition, 1976.

EASTMAN, MARY H. *Index to Fairy Tales, Myths and Legends*. F. W. Faxon Co., Boston, 1926.

Index to Fairy Tales, Myths and Legends. Supplement. F. W. Faxon Co., Boston, 1937–52.

FISHER, MARGERY. *Intent upon Reading*. Brockhampton, Leicester, 1961.

LAVENDER, RALPH. *Myths, Legends and Lore* (Blackwell's Practical Guides for Teachers). Basil Blackwell, Oxford, 1975.

THOMPSON, STITH. *Motif-Index of Folk-Literature*. Five volumes. Revised edition. Rosenkilde and Bagger, Copenhagen, 1955–7.

MT. PLEASANT BRANCH